FYI: This book is an authentic and casual
conversation between you and me.

I0025562

Dedication

This book is dedicated to those…
Those who gave me life…
Those who continue my life…
Those whose lives I've changed…
Those whose lives I will change…
Those who wish me nothing but failure…
Those who laughed…
Those who believe…
Those that will believe…
Those that will apologize…
Those that are ready…
All of Those!

Table of Contents

When Words Create Battles Within Wars

The concept of this book was created by a young man in college who realized his views on situations were different than most individuals in his world. Whenever a conversation of relationships and potential dating situations occurred and he spoke, everyone listened. The words that left his mouth were delivered in such a controversial form due to his straightforward bluntness and inability to think before speaking. He unintentionally would turn a casual conversation into a chaotic conversation that had women against men.

After many unsavory argumentative talks with women, he decided to ask over one-hundred women of different nationalities and backgrounds, "What are the things about men that they don't understand? For example, why do we do or say certain things in certain situations?" From their responses, the questions they had, he took twenty-seven of the questions that stood out the most. And these are the topics this book will cover.

I will be answering these questions with no regards to feelings of the reader. Given that I don't know who you are, do not take anything said in the book personal.

Direct questions regarding marriage or divorce were excluded for the most part due to my lack of experience on that level of a relationship and minimal friends who are in marriages. I'm not able to relate to either topic and want to keep this book as authentic and realistically logical as possible.

Sit·u·a·tion·ship (siCHə'wāSH(ə)n SHip)
- a set of circumstances in which one finds oneself with a significant other in a situation like a relationship but is not a titled secure arrangement

Don't Push Him into a Corner

"Why do Men Freak Out About Commitment?"

Commitment is defined as "the act of binding and dedication to a course of action" according to thefreedictionary.com. The key phrase in the definition I believe is "the act of," because it means that the man or woman must make a choice to bind or dedicate themselves to someone else. Therefore, he or she must make the decision to put themselves in a situation to begin the dating process. If enough time passes by, then the man will be comfortable in this situation; especially if the physical aspects of kissing and sexual activities occur on a regular basis. At this point the man is in his comfort zone. He should have no problem with the ideal situation of great conversation, fun dates, sexual benefits, and waking up next to somebody he enjoys spending time with.

This is the first layer of comfort that the woman should begin to value. The man is open to going out in public with the woman on a regular basis and, at some point, his friends and her friends know about each other. If the comfort level for her has reached the level of her speaking of him to her parents, and the man hasn't provided the "security title" of a girlfriend, then one day the woman will probably bring up a question 99% of men never want to hear. (That's a solid guesstimation with no studies or facts found to back up the %, but you get the point). That question is, "Where are we going with this?" Let me paint you a picture of what that question has now done:

The woman has now backed the man into a corner he does not want to be in, and only a couple scenarios can now occur from this. This is one of the worst places a man can be, in the corner with an ultimatum that can change everything--the situation continuing to go well, or go downhill from there. A man will either tell the truth, or lie in this situation because he doesn't want the good times to stop, typically. But sometimes he chooses to dismiss himself. In his terrible mental corner, a hidden door now appears that will allow him to exit and just run away from it all.

He is looking at the relationship and evaluating everything that has taken place since you have started dating and spending time together. He might be done hanging out with other girls, but this extra amount of pressure now has the man thinking, "I'm having a great time, but I either decide to give her the title and take this relationship to the next level towards marriage…Or do I make the choice of ending the situationship/relationship because I'm not ready?"

The possibility of him just saying, "I'm done!" has a very slim chance of occurring. The only reason a man would exit the situationship at that moment is because he knows he is not ready for a real relationship and doesn't want to lead her on anymore. The next scenario, if he doesn't give the girlfriend title, would be to make her feel more secure about their situation. He gives a bullshit answer like, "I don't see why we need titles to know what the situation is when things are already going great." That translates to: "I like you, but I don't want the titled commitment and have to deal with potential changes in our interactions." This leaves it up to the woman now to either ride it out and hope she gets a title eventually, or shortly after she will be keeping her eyes and options open for that next potential boyfriend she desires.

Either scenario, if he doesn't say, "I want to take it to the next level," the chances of the relationship lasting and getting to the point of saying "I do" are almost non-existent. Let's be true to ourselves, how often do you hear of people in a relationship that doesn't have the boyfriend or girlfriend title and suddenly becomes an engaged couple to get married? I'll wait…

Just kidding. We don't have time for that, I need you to get through this book, but you get the point.

Ladies, whatever you do, don't push a man into a corner of making certain decisions--that will always lower the chances of the relationship working. But at the same time, do not settle for someone simply because they are willing to give you the title. Take a second and ask yourself a few important questions: Has he been faithful? Is he respectful? Is he a gentleman[1]? Has he worked on changing things about

---

[1] I believe there are many definitions of this word and will define them later

himself to keep you happy? And has he also been improving you for the better to help you recognize some of your flaws that you are working on? If the answers to all those questions are "yes," don't let it go quite yet. If one or some of those answers are "no" ... well, you decide what you value in the relationship and act accordingly. I'll share a short story about two friends of mine, Sarah and Anna.

I would like to introduce you all to a friend named Sarah. She is a recent college graduate with a Business Marketing degree who lives in Chicago, Illinois. She and I have been good friends for a few years since I moved to Chicago in 2013. We had a brief fling that ended in a great friendship. After we went a few months without speaking to each other, I got a call out of the blue...

Sarah: Am I doing something wrong for guys to not commit to me? You didn't commit to me for your bullshit reasons but this guy I've been dating for the past two months called me a couple days after our last date and said that he thinks we should leave it as friends for now. Why is that?

(Just FYI, he ended the dating situation around mid-November of that year. For people who know me, know that I'll ask questions for necessary information before I give my analysis)

Me: Have you slept with him?

Sarah: Nope.

Me: Do y'all go Dutch when going out?

Sarah: Nope.

Me: How often do you speak?

Sarah: Almost every day.

Me: Do you spend the night together?

Sarah: Occasionally.

Me: When you first started hanging out, did he state he was open to the idea of a committed relationship?

Sarah: No, he just said he was attracted to me when we met and just wanted to spend time. But later admitted he was starting to like me.

Me: He probably had no intention of developing feelings or expected to like you on that level. Over those two months, he realized he really liked you but isn't ready to give you the relationship you deserve. He figured it was time to end things before the holidays kicked in to avoid those awkward conversations at holiday dinners with family asking, "Are you seeing anybody special?"

Sarah later told me after Christmas time that my assumption was right. The guy told her he realized he wasn't ready for commitment, which was coming up next.

Now my acquaintance Anna's story had a very different ending. Anna is a tall beautiful girl that went to college in Alabama, currently twenty-six years old and an assistant manager at a bank in Dallas, Texas. Anna and I originally planned to spend some time together in a potentially more than friendly way, which would have required travel by flight. When I finally moved to Atlanta and got settled with a new job, about three months later…

Me: Hey I hope all has been well, do you want to still come visit me?

Anna: Things are great but that probably shouldn't happen since I've been talking to someone here for the past month, and it may potentially be serious.

Me: It's no problem. We can just remain friends and I'll contact you if I am ever in the area to catch up.

A few months go by, and it's my birthday

Anna: Hey Happy Birthday!

Me: Thanks, how have things been with you? Still dating that guy?

Anna: I am and things are great, but no title yet.

Of course, I had a few more questions, just out of curiosity, and her update is not what I was expecting.

Anna: Well everybody from our family and friends knows we are together, but I'm a bit worried about not having the commitment title for security reasons.

Me: You don't want to be that girl who was on lock without a title and one day it just ends with you feeling stupid for sticking around so long.

Anna: I agree. We even have a few pics with each other on our social media accounts so it's not a secret from the public as well.

Me: Well, if everyone knows, he isn't afraid to post you on a social media, and he treats you well and is respectful, then definitely don't put added pressure on him for a title.

Long story short, about three more months go by and I saw he decided to make it "Facebook official" that they were in a relationship. It has been four months since then as I'm writing this and they are still going strong. So, my takeaway from this is nobody should add pressure for commitment. If it's meant to be it will be. Maybe in a future book they will be married...

◇◇◇

Well it's been about a year since Anna's example story was written. I caught up with her recently in July 2017... she dumped him. According to her...

Anna: He wasn't fulfilling enough. He's a great guy, but I realized I couldn't marry him, ever.

Does the "I Know I'm Ready" Phase Exist?
"When does a man know he is ready for a relationship?"

The interesting thing about this question, is that some men get into relationships for various reasons. The fantasy of, "I'm getting into a relationship with her because there's that X-factor that pulled me in and I found my soulmate at first sight…" that sh*t doesn't happen too often, if ever. Some reasons for men getting into relationships are (not in order of popularity or preference):

1. He doesn't want anyone else to have her physically/sexually.

2. He is tired of being single and decided he wants to see where things could go with the next girl he takes an interest in.

3. He likes her and sees long-term benefits of being with her whether it's financially beneficial or for career connections.

4. After getting to know her through in-depth conversation, he knows that she is the kind of person he wants to be with long-term.

Number 4, I believe, is the best reason to be in a relationship and the most honest reason. For the first three reasons I provided, he would have to be an extremely bold individual to tell a woman that is why he is with her. Later on while editing this book, I thought of another reason:

5. He had a crazy psycho ass ex-girlfriend, and he has found peace in someone else. And he knows, "I would be a complete idiot to *not* commit to her."

Unfortunately, there is no correct answer to this question because there are multiple reasons for people getting into relationships. The true readiness will be established when a man is in the relationship for the right reasons. When he isn't ready for the faithful commitment, he will continue to have the single person mentality and make single's mindset decisions. In a relationship, you will have to change as a person because you must consider the other person. The man will know he is ready when he is in situations where if he were single, he would make a completely different decision. Here are a few examples of situations and the actions that take place if the man is ready for the relationship:

1. A boy's trip/night hanging out with a great ratio number of girls as there are guys and his friends are trying to engage in sexual activities with these girls.

    a. <u>Single Mindset</u>: He might try to get with one of the girls physically or get her contact information for non-networking purposes.

    b. <u>Relationship Ready</u>: He engages in just a casual conversation with the girl while their friends are having "fun."

2. A night out with a group when his significant other is sitting at home and someone in the group knows an after-party spot to go to.

    a. <u>Single Mindset</u>: He might go to the after party with the group and not worry about his significant other.

b. Relationship Ready: He decides that he wants to go home to his girl because he has been out for a while knowing she's all alone. Or he is considerate enough to ask if she needs him, should he stay out or just go home to her, or go home and contact her in the morning.

3. A career opportunity comes up that is great long-term but it would split them apart in distance.

    a. Single Mindset: He accepts the job and doesn't care much to discuss it with his partner on how this will work out long-term.

    b. Relationship Ready: He tells her he will accept it, and plans how they can see each other regularly and budget out to make it work.

These are just a few basic examples of how he will know he is ready to be all-in with the relationship, *after* he is in the relationship. Again, there's no exact right answer but his actions in situations will show his colors.

My former orthodontist told me a story about his dental school buddy who said to him after his girlfriend dumped him during his first year of grad school, "I'm going to live this single life until I can't take it anymore." I had to ask him when he settled down. He said he was about thirty-three years old and after a wild Miami party weekend, he knew he was done being single. He had finished dental school, started making great money, traveled the world, and even apparently made it his goal to sleep with a different woman in every country he visited over those years. Something about the trip he took to Miami made him realize he was over the single life... I know. I'm also curious as hell, too, about what happened.

He ended up getting married at thirty-five and started his family at thirty-six. My orthodontist says the only thing he regrets about having a family so late is being out of shape trying to keep up with his kid's energy. I'm going to touch on this topic of waiting until you know you are ready in my next book, *Perfecting Single: How to Remain Single on Purpose with a Purpose.*

Turn Offs
"What characteristics immediately push a man away?"

This is one of those questions that the correct answer depends solely on the individual. I'm going to highlight just a few types of women and how the following two types of men, "The Needer" and "The Equalizer," would view this type of woman. First, let me provide the description of these two men (keeping in mind there are plenty more types -- these are just a couple):

The Needer - This type of man feels like the man's role is not to just be able to provide for his family or significant other, but he also wants to be the only person in the relationship able to do it on that level because he believes it makes him "empowered." This sense of power feeds his ego of knowing that without him, she wouldn't be able to do the same things or live the same lifestyle that he is able to provide. **He wants her to need him.** I'll just call this the typical "old school" way in many parts of the world where the man provides the income, and the woman takes care of the household with cooking, cleaning, and managing the children. Another way to describe this is when a man basically wants a trophy wife. Absolutely nothing is wrong with this if the two people in the relationship are happy with this arrangement.

The Equalizer - This type of man will typically only have his attention held for potential long-term relationships when the woman demonstrates the qualities of his equal. This doesn't mean specifically equal in income but the fact that they both work and want to contribute to the household income as a team effort shows they are both capable of being independent, even while together. This man in a short summary wants someone that doesn't need him for anything financially, only for emotional support and some of that "good loving," if you know what I'm saying.

Let's look at two categories of women and how the Needer and Equalizer view them:

- **Miss Financial Independent:** This woman is not settling for a decent salary/status job. She wants to be that above average woman in her career and live as comfortably as she desires without needing assistance from a man. Her ambition is to be so financially independent she will be able to buy her own home, eat wherever she wants on a regular basis, drive the car of her choice, and spoil herself with gifts without any assistance from a significant other. These women lower the Needer's self-esteem and intimidate him as a man because he knows she doesn't need him for the monetary things in life. He's scared she would leave him and be just fine--which she would if she decides she didn't want to be with him anymore. This woman completes the Equalizer because he believes there's nothing better than a woman that he knows doesn't need him for monetary things, therefore she truly wants him for who he is as a person. He feels more privileged to be hers for those reasons.

- **Gold Digger:** A woman who wants to be with her man all the time because of what he can do for her, not solely on feelings for wanting to see the significant person she "cares about." She knows how to cater to him and his ego, to try to get the things she wants long-term--never having to work long-term. If he commits to her, even temporarily, she will have elevated her lifestyle strictly because he provides her with monetary materialistic things. She is the one that will always have suggestions for date nights or events knowing that she isn't going to spend a dime and looks forward to her "significant other" spoiling her with a gift that she could not get on her own. The Needer might fall for this long-term because he doesn't mind knowing without him, she couldn't live that lifestyle. These women are typically looking to be or give off the vibe that they just want to be a trophy wife and manage the household. The Equalizer does not entertain this woman very long, if at all. He knows that she is looking to do nothing but decrease the bank account and to him, that doesn't provide the type of value to his life that keeps his interest.

◇◇◇

After re-reading the "Gold-Digger" section, I hope there is no misunderstanding. It may come off as if I am inferring that a housewife is a gold-digger, WHICH IS NOT what I am saying. A housewife could be a turn-off to some men but there are different types of housewives. One housewife could be a less proactive wife in the family that has a nanny, chef, housekeeper, accountant, etc. to manage daily operations for the family. Then there are housewives who may do the cleaning, cooking, managing the kids, managing the financial budget, reviewing investment performances, etc. that adds a different type of value that would have cost the family additional income to hire an outside person to provide those services.

For some men who are professional athletes or business owners and work significant hours, a housewife can ease their stress to know that certain aspects of the house are taken care of. All in-preference and lifestyle needs but at the end of the day remember this--housewife or housewife aspirations does NOT mean she is a gold-digger.

I decided to add in just one more type of woman that honestly could grab the attention of the Needer and the Equalizer in a positive way:

- **The Free-Spirit:** There are multiple definitions based on perspectives of "free-spirited" people but to stick with a published definition of the word, I entered "Free-spirit definition" into a Google search. One definition provided says "independent and not constrained by convention," which is the one I want to focus on for now. Basically, anybody who doesn't care to abide by social norms or being "regular or typical" in the view of others is a free spirit. Let's be completely honest--there are some women that are free-spirited sexually in the sense of sleeping with any guy she wants or finds attractive if the opportunity presents itself. By definition, that is a free-spirit because conventionally by society's definition she would be looked at as a slut, hoe, whore, etc. That is unfortunately a double standard for men. In her mind, she is not a slut. She's just living her life freely. Overall, we cannot judge them because we don't walk on water, but those "free-spirits" typically aren't appealing to the Needer or Equalizer unless she has something very specific about her that they learn keeps their attention. Most men who want to commit to one person typically won't want to know or hear about the significant other they want for themselves being shared with someone else. Both the Needer and the Equalizer could be turned off by this sexually free-spirited woman.

In summary, you can see that the Needer and the Equalizer typically have complete opposite views on the women in the first two categories listed but to each his own. Not one type of man or woman is better than the other. We all just have our preferences. Below are just a few more turn-offs to some men.

- **Broken Women:** The woman who has had her heart broken by a cheater and now doesn't trust any man. So, she constantly contacts him to see what he is doing and who he is with. Her insecurity will push many great men away before they even have a chance to see where the relationship could go.

- **Boring Sex:** I've met many people who have rushed into sexual activity and some of the men unfortunately decided not to pursue contact with a girl afterwards due to the boringness she brought to the bedroom. There could have potentially been a different outcome if that aspect wasn't rushed. He could have taught her some things if he took the time to get to know her, or maybe she was tired already from the day's activities called life. Always a possibility that he is boring to her, too, so she didn't want to put in quality effort.

- **The Talker:** The woman who not only doesn't shut-up about anything that adds no value to life, but the woman who talks about a lot of people in either a bad way or provides details on other individuals' lives that probably shouldn't be shared. A lot of gossip can have a man conclude that she may share his personal business that he may want to keep private.

I have quite a few friends on either end of the spectrum as Needers and Equalizers. One of my great friends Johnathan--he works as a chemical engineer--is the definition of a Needer. One day over brunch, the topic came up about people's preferences of household income in the future and contributions and fund allocations, and he just became very adamant saying...

Johnathan: I don't want any woman I'm dating to make what I'm making or more. That would make me feel like I'm not a man because she's bringing in more financial contribution to the house.

Me: ***Looks at him like he's crazy*** Teamwork makes the dream work. And if something happened to you, why not have backup income that's equal or greater to keep you afloat until you're back on your feet with a new opportunity?

Of course, neither of us are better than one another and we are entitled to our opinions but the most important thing is that whether a man is a Needer or an Equalizer, just be sure you're happy in your relationship and dating situations.

Problems with Recognition of the Truth

"How will she know if he is really interested?"
"If he waits for sex, is it because it's real or patience for penetration?"

Do any women reading this have some friends that will give each other advice, saying, "If he is real, then, he will wait for sex," and "You shouldn't have to open your legs for a man to want to get to know you and spend his time with you"? I'm an honest believer in that statement. All men who aren't virgins or--for religious purposes--"born again virgins" are going to want sex with the person they are dating, hanging out with, or whatever the hell your situationship title is. If he loses interest because he can't have the "dessert of choice" after taking you on a date, then you two aren't meant to be together, period. I'll just reiterate it because I'm sure we have all met someone who would sleep with a guy to try to keep him around. If he can't wait and you want to wait, the sh*t just won't work out. Proceed.

There isn't one correct answer to these two questions because everybody is different. You have some women who have been single so long, she might be able to convince herself very early on that the next guy who takes her out and shows interest might be real when he could simply just be enjoying his time with her with no commitment goals. I would agree that not having sexual interactions is the simplest step to see if he is interested in *you* and not interested in only being inside you. Of course, some women reading this are thinking, "That's stupid because I have my sexual needs that need to be met." In your life, you will do what is best for you. But if that method of opening your legs early on has resulted in you being single over and over again,...can't do the exact same thing and expect another outcome. Anybody else agree?

As I said before, not many men will look at a woman and say, "She is so beautiful I just can't wait to get to know her personality." I promise that has never been said by a man. Now this does bring on the issue of knowing if he is waiting for sex because he likes you, or just taking his time to get what his original goal was from sexual attraction. Only way to guarantee it is real is if the stipulations for sex are:

1. Must be in a titled committed relationship
2. Must be married

If a man heard that from day one, it would save some women a lot of wasted time talking to guys. Well, as long as the woman sticks to her requirements and doesn't give up the goods for "good behavior" early on. She will have a man that is truly there for her. Does the "I Know I'm Ready" phase exist? It does, but it is so unique to every individual man that there's not enough space in a chapter, a book, or even a series of books to lay out every scenario when a man knows he is ready for the real relationship.

A sadly entertaining story with this situation is about a new friend I've made named Jaclyn. Jaclyn is a nurse in North Carolina. While she was in college, a guy she met wanting to "date her" was the assumption. He would always ask her out, and she would say no. Years go by, and he had a girlfriend. When that ended, he would try to get with her again, still offer declined. Now it's been a few years after graduation and she decided to give him a shot. He took her out on a few dates and things seemed to have been good for 3 months and then suddenly, his communication got worse and she gave up and ended the fling. She told me:

Jaclyn: I slept with him within the first week after the 2nd date because I thought if he was this persistent so long he must really want to date me and see how it goes.

Me: I know of some other guys who stay persistent or on the radar for years. And did it for sex and they said those text and calls overtime were worth it.

I personally believe she fell victim to this, especially after she told me his main source of income was as a party promoter so she knew he spent time with a lot of women just because of the nature of the business. She took it as a lesson learned and plans to wait until she's in an official titled committed relationship before she has sex again. As she puts it: "Too many guys are just full of crap these days and don't want honest exclusive commitment." I wonder how many of my current readers who are female or male agree...

Quantity vs. Quality

"Why do men like easy sex over a woman with 'values'?"

This double standard occurs in all phases of life. From high school throughout college, and even post-graduation living in the "real world" seems to have the same outcome. If a man can have sex with multiple girls, he is "the man;" he has "the juice" and has "game;" he is an admired "player" by some people. If a woman has sex with multiple men, she's considered a "whore," "slut," "easy," "loose," or "has no self-respect" according to typical society. It is not right to categorize men and women differently for the exact same actions but that is just the way it is and it will never change unfortunately. Get over it. The question that needs to be asked is why do some men want to sleep with multiple women? Just penetrating at every opportunity with someone he doesn't care about or doesn't want to be in a relationship with at that moment. When he could stick with one great woman who would treat him like a king, which should encourage him to treat her like his queen, right?

There are a few factors that can make a man want to spend his time "inside" multiple women:

1. **Lack of Readiness:** Sometimes a man is just not ready to stick with one woman, no matter how great she is. And he doesn't want to lie to himself or the "main" woman in his life. Better for a man to run free doing whatever he wants than "selling her the dream" of love and commitment. I personally believe that makes him significantly more of a boy than a man regardless of age if

he is playing games. Again, that's if he is playing games and not being truthful about his intentions, not the action itself to be with multiple women.

2. **Immaturity:** If a man is trying to have more girls than options of beers at the brewery and making multiple girls try to feel like they have the value and exclusiveness of a Bugatti Veyron ($1 Million+ car), he is just stupid and immature, especially if he's past the age of twenty-five. Get it together or at least start to get it together fellas if your age is at minimum half-way to fifty. There is a point in life when it's time to stop playing games and just be honest with yourself and whoever you choose to interact with to potentially cross the physical line. Unfortunately, lying has been working so long it's hard to break the habit.

3. **Age (potentially):** How many years a man has lived potentially plays a factor in when he hits that stage of wanting a girl with qualities or just want to increase his "body count." Most men are not truly "ready" to even potentially settle down in his mid-to-late twenties. Any time before that, most guys are lying to themselves thinking they are ready because they have a great girl, their friends are getting married, or pressure from family members directly or indirectly. They tend to forget that just because she is great, doesn't mean he is ready. A particular age doesn't guarantee being ready.

4. **The Upbringing:** If a man during his childhood saw his father cheating on his mother, or if the parents weren't together and he saw the father with different women, he is likely to go down one of two paths. The first path, he will mirror his father and want to have many options all the time. I believe this is more likely to occur if he has a great relationship with his father. Studies show that if a child admires a parent of the same sex, they will likely strive to be like them[2]. Path two, he will see how his father made those women feel and go the opposite path and will be a one-woman man; more likely to occur if the relationship with the parent wasn't the greatest and despises trying to be like them when they were growing up. Unfortunately, some men never had a father around to learn from, and those boys and are forced to grow up figuring it out all on their own, unless they find another influential person in their life to show them the ropes.

5. **Social Status:** The title a man has in his daily life plays a major influence on if he wants to use his title to improve the quantity or quality of the "company he keeps." Studies show that many women go through a phase when open to dating, that they are attracted to men who have some form of title that shows him as being above average compared to others. These titles could range from being a jock, to being member of the debate team, to a politician, member of a

[2] ***Being a Role Model: The Pearl and the Peril*- Audrey Krisbergh, Certified Parenting Educator**

fraternity, a business man on the rise, an entertainer in the music or film arts, etc. What women fail to realize is that there are many more women with the same mindset so he is given options immediately. Job titles and industry typically have a correlation with how much money he makes, and some women are gold diggers at heart without even realizing it. When a woman knows he is financially stable, she may potentially end up dropping her standards from keeping her legs closed to "giving it up." But, remember there are other women doing the same thing for him so try to show the qualities you have, not just be a part of the quantity.

These five factors combined contribute to a man's decision to be a man-whore, player, or *pimp*. It isn't the woman's fault; it's the man's decision at the end of the day. Here are stories of men who are prime examples of some of the 5 factors listed above:
Oh sh*t, wait, I literally just thought of this other situation right now on June 6th, 2017 at 6:18pm to be the 6th and final potential reason why a man can enjoy Quantity over Quality and I bet we all have met at least one man who is the emotionally shattered man.

6. **Emotionally Shattered**: You don't hear about him on a regular basis, but there is that man who had his heart broken by a woman and he loses his mind! Completely explodes or implodes out of pure raw emotions for the woman that he wanted to be with forever. He has potentially made sacrifices for her, depending on how much time they were together, and when she left him, he went on an uncontrolled rampage to hurt other women emotionally. His heart has turned black and has no regards to feelings because he's in his feelings. Damn, I feel bad for the women that became victim to this

type of emotional angry man. Ladies and gentlemen, if you believe you became victim to this over-emotional ass borderline crazy man or are friends with one, tell him to go buy a copy of this book to read about himself in this chapter. Alright back to the story telling.

Meet Steven. He's a thirty-five-year-old attorney at a financial services company in the D.C., Maryland, Virginia area who has been single since he was twenty-four. Every weekend he looks forward to going out and meeting new girls just to try to have sex with them as soon as possible. He will at times have a girl he considers his "main girl" who he will take out on dates occasionally but he knows he will not commit to her or any other girl exclusively. I can probably guesstimate he has been with well over 100 women and this is just a combination of lack of being ready and a bit immature. Now his personal reasons are, he claims, that he just isn't ready--which is true, but I personally believe there is something else he hasn't fulfilled and he's filling that void with multiple women. I'm not a psychologist but one thing is clear, he just isn't ready. What do you think?

Now Steven isn't an extremely high paid lawyer so his natural status may look like an average Joe in the corporate world, but meet Brandon. He is the PR spokesperson for the largest utility company in the Northeast, which has him at a well above average income and travel benefits for work. Typically, companies use people who are deemed physically attractive to address the general public, and when I met Brandon, he showed me his "rolodex" of women he had as options. I'll admit, it was a very impressive lineup based on their images and the diversity of the "portfolio." He even said, "I travel a lot, I meet a lot of women for work, and I'm not sure if I'll settle down while I'm in the public eye speaking at conferences a lot with all the temptation available." Now I believe immaturity plays a role in this with lack of readiness, but his social status and income attracts women to him. He believes that for him to settle down, he will need to be less in the public eye.

If only women united in some form of a secret society with a purpose to have men treat women and their bodies with the respect they deserve, a one-strike policy would be ideal for change. I'll come back to this idea later, but for now focus on developing your qualities, because realistically the scenario of women uniting to have men treat them how they believe they all deserve, will never happen. The way so many women intentionally, or unintentionally, compete with each other, this secret society probably wouldn't last long enough to achieve the goal. Throw in the fact some women never received the love they probably needed from their fathers growing up, and naturally yearn for it from a man, which could end with them becoming victims of the immature game-playing man.

Let's Talk About Sex

"How often does sex cross a man's mind?"

The answer to this question will, of course, be influenced whether the man is a virgin or not. I would have to say that, from a non-virgin's perspective, we think about it a lot. Unfortunately, there isn't any scientific evidence I could find or heard of that backs up this next statement, but I believe we think about sex less than women. I'm not going that route though for the explanation. When a man looks at a woman he is attracted to, it doesn't matter if it is a mutual friend he meets, a lady at the mall, a co-worker, or even a classmate. If he is attracted to her, he has thought about having sex with her. That does not mean he is going to act on it, but the curiosity is there temporarily.

I'm not saying he takes his imagination as far as really fantasizing and picturing it, but in a very casual way he's thought, "She looks good enough to have sex with." I have never met or think there is one man on this planet who looks at an attractive woman and says to himself, "Wow, she is beautiful. I want to get to know her verbally!" That sh*t just doesn't happen. Throughout the process of trying to get to know the woman physically, he will potentially develop feelings towards her through verbal communication. Sometimes a man is forced to wait for the physical contact. If he doesn't really like her or have an interest in getting to know her beyond the physical interaction, he will move-on right after sex, which is extremely disrespectful and unfortunately happens. This leads many women to ask this question:

"Why do men like to rush into sex?"

To the general public, women who are deemed "classy" have morals, respect for their bodies, and want to have sex with a particular man because they "value themselves" and will not just let any man have that pleasure with her. It's a significant emotional bond that she wants to share with an exclusive individual. Unfortunately for you ladies, to the majority of men, sex is just a verb. During penetration, we aren't thinking about the fact that we are having sexual relations with this beautiful unique woman, we are just doing something that feels good. Better yet, it feels great! Depending on how long he had to wait for the "feeling," he could be thinking this is like that moment in the game of Monopoly that he wasn't allowed to pass Boardwalk, "I'm finally able to pass go! I can collect $200!"

I met this guy named Jacob, a former investment banker who is now the CEO of a food packaging company. He was always bragging about the beautiful girls he slept with and explained that after a long-time relationship ended, he took out 40 girls on dates over a 10-month time frame and enjoyed the "benefits" with many of them. This man did eventually hit the wall of single life. He settled down, got married, and said he has no regrets of his past.

That is why many men can cheat on the women they love with a girl that has no emotional value or any significance to us. Sex is just a verb. It is like going on a jog, playing basketball, or taking the dog for a walk...without the "pay-off" of course. Sex is just an activity. I'm not saying it is right for a man to cheat on his woman, but if he does say "I still love you," after getting caught cheating, he potentially means it. If a man happens to cheat, the woman could be using bad judgment and put up with it, hoping he stops. Unless you know your trust is completely gone, be logical and leave him if that would make you happy long term. Logically it is simple as that, but I know some people use their feelings to make decisions and end up getting hurt even more. If a man can cheat and keep his woman if she catches him, it is a slim to none chance that he won't ever cheat or potentially be in that situation again. He realized he could do that and still be able to keep you around afterwards.

Hopefully he understands that by cheating, he is going to cause you pain and will think of keeping you happy going forward. Now if there is an understanding between the couple in the relationship/situationship that the man is going to have the freedom to cheat, then that's just their arrangement (I don't even know if that could truly be considered cheating if it is an agreement). I've honestly heard of some situations where the woman is so fascinated with the quality of his sexual performance, she will be hypnotized by it to the point where it affects her logical thought process when he has cheated and tries to stay around. She just thinks "Damn, he is *laying pipe* so well I might as well hold-on to it since I get serviced the most." Sometimes there is an opposite situation though.

When some couples begin to have sex on a regular basis, this can lead to a sensitive topic that men may never know--If the woman isn't being satisfied...what does she do? I conducted a study when I lived in Chicago of random individuals who are in relationships or situationships I met from group chats, co-workers, and friends. The results showed 45% of individuals, of the 100 couples surveyed, were not completely sexually satisfied with their partner. I avoided asking married individuals. I have no clue what marriage life is like as I stated earlier. Besides, it would be awkward to look at someone I know of and think, "Wow, they go home to their spouse and have boring sex."

This is something that can be overlooked by some women, but other women may feel tempted to find the adventure they are hungering for to satisfy their appetite. Leading into another question produced from my survey of questions from women:

"How should a woman tell her man he is not satisfying her sexually?"

If a man and his woman are in a location where "the magic happens" but there aren't any "abracadabra" moments, then there is a problem. How do you tell a magician his show sucked and his illusions were poorly fabricated while you acted like you were impressed with his talents? This will be a very difficult conversation to have, but the most important thing a woman can do is keep this a private matter. If there's no one else in bed with you, then nobody should know about this issue. If a man's ego gets hurt from his woman and her friends knowing about it too, it just makes the situation a lot worse. I had to do some extensive private research to find the answers for this situation. Let's look at a few scenarios that can lead to the resolution of this issue.

- **Direct Approach:** If a woman is extremely blunt and says she isn't sexually satisfied, his reaction will most likely be either asking for her advice on what the problem is, or he will be offended and point out her flaws to try to make himself feel more secure. It is a very immature move, but he is clearly trying to protect his self-confidence on the outside by firing back. Meanwhile on the inside he feels like he just got cut from the varsity team, demoted from the starting quarterback to the water-boy on the roster. Now another thought could be "Okay, I need to avoid being put on the bench. When the next game comes around I will be beyond ready and perform like Michael Jordan in the 4th quarter."

- **Catering Approach:** Another way to take pressure off him, the woman could ask him if there is anything she can do to keep him stimulated and help him perform better. It is a reverse psychological tactic that will make him believe he can perform better if she can bring some extra to the show that potentially keeps him significantly more attentive to her and ends up satisfying her better in a shorter amount of time.

- **3-Strikes Approach:** This last scenario is the best suggestion because this method will allow you to have this discussion by being discrete with your words. He will have no clue you're "schooling" him. Before you potentially doubt his "talents" for the long run, do it with him at least three times before you pull out the clipboard and coach him. If a baseball player gets 3 strikes before he is struck out and heads back to the dugout to regroup and prepare for his next time "up at bat," then the man you are having sex with should have the same opportunity. These are a few potential scenarios for why he hasn't hit that ass like a homerun in the 9th inning:

- It could have been a while since he was "swinging the bat," so his technique could be a little rusty and just needs to get warmed up.

- After a long day or night working, he might not have fuel in the tank or the energy to prepare for his second job of the day— "to be a plumber and lay pipe." If you know your partner is tired at night from working, maybe try doing it in the morning after you are both rested. It's another form of "breakfast in bed."

- Possibly, he is just a lazy selfish asshole who genuinely wasn't worried about pleasing you because he knew he was satisfied with his performance. He assumes you'll still be there for another round.

- There's also a possibility he just isn't experienced and doesn't know quite how to please you in that way.

My first suggestion is to boost his ego using comments when he is stroking in a manner you enjoy. Comments like "Ahhh just like that," and "Yes, don't stop." He has been coached to "run that play" every time the ball is in his hands.

Now when a woman doesn't have the opportunity to make those comments to boost his morale genuinely, after the game ends and you took an "L" (loss), it's time for the "locker room talk" (the coaching moment after a bad game has occurred). In a calm tone, you can tell him you have a couple of questions. One of them is, "What is your masturbation schedule or how often do you beat your meat when I'm away?" .... I know it sounds awkward as hell, but this could work. Do not skip this chapter, because this could be life-changing. Now his eyes might open wide and he will tell you, then likely respond with, "What about *your* schedule?" Ladies, tell him your schedule so that now you can slide in a response along the lines of, "In my sex life I have explored and figured out there are some things that I really truly enjoy." For the first time in a while, without having sex, you will have his full and complete attention. Now he is thinking, "What the hell is she about to say about her sex life? I better pay attention and listen for once. ***then he grabs a beer in his mind***"

Now his interest has escalated faster than a spaceship at lift off. Ladies, if you receive a response like, "Oh really? Like what?" -- Congrats, you are about to tell him everything you like that he hasn't done and he is keeping thorough detailed mental notes like a student sitting in a professor's office hours asking about how to get extra credit after finals. Please be careful though with how much "work and experience you unveil" to him; you don't want to crush his hopes with information overload. There's always another time or semester to provide more extra credit opportunities to him if you know what I'm saying.

Once he has his extra credit requirements, he may even provide you some suggestions on how you can help him out by "delivering the content during class effectively." Ladies, if you are listening carefully, know you are a great *professor* who will bring out the best abilities in her student, and he may not need to get "extra credit" to get the grades you both want. This is a win-win for both of you. You're welcome.

Check out this story about my friend Angela in Miami. We caught up during a trip there not too long ago. She asked about my dating life and I asked about hers. She brought up a guy who works in marketing for a professional team there in Miami and how she thought he was a great person. After a couple months of waiting she decided to see what the sex was like. The next day he asked her how his performance was and she responded with, "I was expecting better." I had that bug out eyes emoji look on my face because this was the pure definition of the Direct Approach.

Me: Daaaaaaamn! What did he say to that?

Angela: He said "Well I had a long day and was a bit tired so I wasn't on my A game, but glad you told me."

     They dated for about 4 more months and then it ended. My guess is she gave him another opportunity. But assuming they worked out that issue, it wouldn't save the relationship from whatever issues they had that resulted in a break-up. As a man, I can't imagine how I would react if a woman said that to me. Fellas, how would you react if the woman you're currently constantly with or last slept with said that?

     Back to the important point I mentioned earlier, keeping this matter as private as possible would be great for the relationship because I know that not all, but some women, do talk about their sexual experience with their partner to other female or male friends. Try to keep it quiet unless you have something to brag about it, but don't project his negative sexual abilities. Now I did just say all that after sharing an entertaining story about somebody I know but that's just to provide a solid example. Until now I haven't told anybody because it wasn't necessary to bring up.

Lack of Sensitivity
"Why are men insensitive?"
"Why don't men talk about and express their feelings?"

Many actions of men and women have been pre-decided/conditioned by society from a very early age. The world we live in has made unwritten laws of what men and women should do and how they should act. Looking at this from an entertainment view, movies that contain action, bullets, explosions, and inappropriate humor that would be considered disrespectful to women or disgusting, are typically more popular with men. This social construct has conditioned boys to not express emotions or be sensitive. That's why the chick flick categories exist.

Men like to leave the sensitive and emotional conversations for the women. Not saying we do not have feelings and emotions, but we typically are more selective of when we show them. Sometimes we don't expect to show them and that's when they can become out of control at a breaking point of an argument or misunderstanding. It will take more time for men to show their true feelings than women usually but sometimes the feelings on display aren't completely honest. Some men choose their words carefully and hold back the complete truth to avoid any potential reactions of hers that could be good or bad. One thing that does get on a lot of men's nerves is when women try to bring the emotions out when we clearly aren't trying to take a conversation in that direction. That's like trying to force a turtle to come out of their shell with a pair of tweezers-- it will cause more damage than intended. The further you reach to get him out of his comfort zone, the easier it is to hold it in. When a man gets more comfortable with his female counterpart, he will at some point start to show and tell his feelings on his own.

Ladies, ask yourself this question: Would you really want a man to be more sensitive? I would like a woman to think about how she truly is and weigh out the pros and cons of being a woman in general regarding emotions and reactions. Would you want to date someone so like you in those aspects? If that answer is no, then that would let you know that working through the "insensitive" issues is just the nature of being with someone knowing that things will not always be smooth and will help you grow as a team. Whether you're officially committed in a relationship, beginning the dating process, or in a situationship, you will grow. From a scientific perspective, this is just a difference in hormones.

The testosterone vs. estrogen battle has a significant influence. In a study published for **DiscoveryHealth.com**, "Estrogen and Testosterone Hormones," men produce 6-8 mg of testosterone a day while women produce only 0.5 mg a day. Men produce far lower amounts of estrogen compared to women which influences emotions correlating to the way we will react to different situations.

Between the genetic makeup of our primary hormones and society's unwritten rules, men in-general will never be as sensitive as women. The genders will not see eye-to-eye very often. The only way you can potentially achieve that level of understanding as a team is through effective communication on both sides.

Side note: During the brief research related to testosterone levels, an article by Turnham TC, Harvard Business School associate, wrote in 2003 "Horm Behav." A study was conducted that showed men who were open to or in romantic relationships, produced 21% lower testosterone levels than single men. This is a decent indicator of why more women are looking for or open to relationships than men are as a priority, due to lower testosterone levels.

An example of how social constructions can hurt dating situations is a lady named Jasmine. I met her on a plane heading to Miami a few years ago. We somehow got on the topic of dating and her current situationship. I mentioned I had drafted a book answering questions about why men do or say certain things in different situations. She was interested in this particular chapter when I showed her the list of questions my book answers.

She proceeded to say, "Society really damages expectations and perceptions" all because the guy she was dating at the time was extremely insensitive according to her. Her example of this was when she told him about her sister having a miscarriage due to stress of finding out her husband had been cheating on her when he was on business trips. His reaction was basically non-existent. He said, "that is very unfortunate," and was ready to continue another conversation while he could tell she was really upset by this tragic event. Apparently, his parents raised him with the belief that as a man, he can never be soft, ever. He must remain strong through all situations.

She believes he was mentally conditioned not to express feelings of sympathy or empathy and that just made him seem inhumane. My reaction to the story was really imagining if that happened to somebody close to me. I would keep them in prayers and hope that her brother-in-law seriously reevaluates his decisions going forward. She told me before we exited the plane that her next dating situation, she would really try to see what values the man has received from his parents or parental figures who raised him before she gets as emotionally invested.

I Heard You...But I Wasn't Listening
"Why are men bad at communicating?"
"Why are men passive listeners?"

The day ladies understand that there is a very short limit of time to communicate your point, before we lose full concentration and are forced to provide a response to expedite to the end of the conversation, communication between both parties won't be as meaningful. Men want to hear the specific details-- who, what, when, where, how, and why! The following phrases will have a man hit auto-pilot as soon as possible: "I was feeling..." or "You made me feel like...." The beginning of those phrases means it will be a longer conversation than necessary, and we would much rather enjoy life than listen to whatever you're going to say next. It's almost as bad as nails scratching on a chalkboard. We would rather watch paint dry on the wall than hear that crap. Keep calm and don't take the use of the "c" word personal. We don't actually think your feelings and thoughts have the value level as low as poop.

Any man that has heard these phrases, knows this conversation is going to basically be about something that he has done wrong, and everything is his fault. Our first thought is, "What is the best way of getting through this conversation without feeling my soul being drained of life?" ...Okay, I'm being a little dramatic but you get the point. Ladies, if your man says the following phrases, he just wants to end the conversation before it truly begins:

- "I completely agree."
- "Okay."
- "You know what, you're right."

- "Do you need some money to go shopping or go get a manicure & pedicure?"

I'm not suggesting all men do this and try to speed through a conversation to avoid conflict, but for the ones that do--he didn't hear a damn word you said. He is just glad he finished the conversation with no tears or bloodshed. Ladies, imagine you ran into a woman or man you dislike with a passion (a better phrase than *hate*) and you have mutual friends. You have to be with them temporarily during a day or night out, just hoping you don't have to say anything to them the whole time being around them. That anxiety is how we feel when we have those emotional conversations about how you feel and the things we need to do to make you feel better. Just want to be cordial to avoid conflict and increase the peace.

To all you beautiful women that we cannot live without, please every now and then take the time and just simply shut up. As opposed to taking shots and trying to get your point across first, try asking questions to make us respond in full sentences where we must think about it. We will be more engaged in the conversation and it will potentially end with a better resolution, though never guaranteed.

An old friend of mine from home, Garrett once told me his (now ex-) girlfriend was being deemed "emotional." Before the conversation ended, he said "Babe you're right, so let me know if you need to get your nails done before you go to your friend's event tonight. I got it if you want me to. I'm sorry." He said she calmly finished the argument in two minutes and then proceeded to get ready. He swears this was an *investment* for quiet time alone with a bottle of whiskey and relaxation. He said it was worth every dollar to sacrifice his pride and not stand up to her in that moment. Now this is not a recommendation for what men should do to get out of arguments or conversations, but it was funny the way he explained the story to me.

In some situations, us being passive listeners isn't a good thing. But in those moments, women should embrace the control they have with very little resistance, especially when it comes to women who seem to love being in control of most situations and outcomes. Sometimes being passive can lead to serious consequences with miscommunication. This is probably why the following question made this list...

Need Space vs. Need a Break

"Why don't men tell their woman that they just need alone time without shutting down?"

Many relationships get to a point where it seems whatever the woman wants, she gets. If some women aren't happy, they will argue, scream, and eliminate the "benefits" the man receives from her, just to get her way. Over time, a man might just give up arguing and just say "Okay/alright." Ladies, one thing you must learn is that you aren't the only one who will sometimes go silent and have a storm brewing that leads you to make a decision that can catch the other person off guard, such as leaving or cheating. If all you hear is "Okay/alright," that is one of the few warning signs from *some* men.

The phrase "Okay/alright" can be translated at times to be "I don't feel like arguing about this right now, I'm annoyed with you, or I'm tired of hearing your mouth." Unfortunately, to keep the peace, he will just keep the phrase shorter. Now as a man, I don't believe he should necessarily stand up against his woman to get what he wants, but he should negotiate whatever the situation is and find a common ground to agree on as a team. If a man is getting fed up with her wanting control of the couple's activities--going on trips, the date night movies or restaurants, where they spend the holidays together, the career path the man should be pursuing, etc.-- this is the beginning of the end of the relationship. When a man hits his limits, it's a wrap and a good chance of no return to the positive situation it was before. He abandons ship, at least mentally.

My good friend Olivia had this happen to her over a year ago. Olivia had a boyfriend and they had been together for about a year. She thought things were going great. She was going on the type of dates she wanted, received little gifts at her request, and being a little spoiled to an extent. She suddenly had this relationship-related post on Instagram and Facebook basically saying, "I don't know what's going on. I thought things were great but all of a sudden he wants to take a break!" Men use the phrase "We need to take a break," to mean, "I care about you, but I need some time to explore my other options." I think it is safe to assume that ladies would much rather hear the phrase "I need some space," to say, "I care about you, but you are just a little too all over my case. We need to figure out what's going to work for both of us and I just want to clear my head but not lose you." Feel free to go to my website www.Aristonteleo.com and give everyone your definition of "We need a break!"

Another example of this is my friend Lilly. Lilly is an Australian immigrant who's working on her MBA. She was dating this guy named Harry who was working on his law degree in another state. The long-distance factor didn't keep them from staying in touch on a consistent basis with video chats and phone calls. One day, Lilly and I caught up over pizza, and she brought up that she was recently single. I thought they were all good, but then she told me that one day on the phone he said, "You really drain me." I know, I was just like you thinking the same thing hearing that…. "Well damn."

Apparently, her thought process was, "Since we are both very busy with limited time to talk, when we have time, we should talk on the phone." His thought process was, "I really don't want to talk to you every day on the phone because I really dread just talking on the phone to talk. I would rather talk with purpose only." He never expressed this to her because he wanted to please her and give her what she needed from him to make her happy. Because it was bottled up, it exploded with the phrase "You really drain me," which was the downfall of the relationship and led to the breakup a week later.

My opinion is anyone who is dating somebody and doing something they don't like to do strictly to please their partner should have a conversation regarding the matter and come to a compromise. Just effectively communif*ckingcate and things will be great! I know I know, that's way easier said than done. But give it a try.

Unfortunately, these situations were examples of terrible communication on the man's part and not addressing the issue as soon as it started to affect him. There's no direct answer, unfortunately, as to why some men don't give the woman the heads up about how they are feeling; too many different people, personalities, and backgrounds to analyze and provide them all.

Get Your Life Together

"Why aren't men very assertive with their life decisions?"

When I received this question, I was a bit puzzled at first. I asked the women who had this question what they mean by "assertive," and in what ways. Their responses were, "EVERYTHING!" Apparently-- remember this is all in perspective, there's a high volume of men today who are not as confident or do not show their confidence in many aspects of their life. Or maybe those women have bad luck and tend to attract men who are missing the self-confidence quality. The range of events where some women have had an issue with a man not being assertive are: deciding on the type or specific woman he wants, following his passion instead of being miserable in a job he doesn't like, lack of short-term and long-term goals, and failure to plan to be successful. I personally think that too many women are committing to guys because they see "potential" when he clearly doesn't have it together and that potential isn't "high-quality potential."

The world is a difficult place. Society's system we grow up in is far from perfect. They never tell you as a kid that if you follow your passion and not only work hard at it, but develop a plan of milestones to reach it, you could have the financial satisfaction and enjoy every day in your hobby, not just a job. The system tells you that you should go to college by whatever means necessary, get a degree, get a job, and that's the beginning of "success." Growing up in this system doesn't exactly let you be who you are, which slows down the process of figuring out who you are and ultimately what makes you happy.

I truly believe that is the reason why some people are so indecisive in life and aren't as assertive because they don't know who they are yet. They are in the process of trying to figure it out as time goes by and decide which path of life is best for them. This unknown lost feeling internally will affect his confidence in situations dealing with adversity.

Instead of asking a man to be more confident and why he can't make a decision, why not ask, "Where do you see yourself five years from now?" After he gives his response, ask him to elaborate on his plan to get there. His response should be a significant indicator if he knows who he is, what he wants, and (most importantly) what he *doesn't* want in his life, and if his plan sounds attainable.

Remember, every man is different and could have other factors thrown in such as personal background and how they were raised, the environment they were raised in, and their exposure to life events that affect their life choices. I would just urge women to not use this as a deciding factor to end a current situation with somebody, unless it makes you unhappy to even be with them or if you feel like it is slowing you down on your personal path to success. I personally believe people in a dating situation or full commitment should enhance each other. That's the best indication of a relationship going the right direction, just my opinion. Let other readers know your opinion on indications of a great relationship in the comments section of this book's website.

I wonder how many people could say they dated a boy like who my friend Allison did, or maybe some of the men reading this have a friend like Jerry[3], Allison's ex. First let's analyze Allison and Jerry's backgrounds:

- Allison and Jerry are both from Maryland and started dating senior year of high school.

- Allison went to college in North Carolina. Jerry went to school near home in Maryland.

- Jerry dropped out after freshman year to pursue a music career because it was his passion. Allison was a great girlfriend and supported his dream.

---

[3] **To be honest I don't remember her ex's name, but Jerry came to mind while typing.**

The long-distance factor is now between them during their relationship. Allison loves him and wants to see him be successful, but she hates that when friends ask about her boyfriend. She feels slightly embarrassed to say he has dropped out of college to pursue music and lives at his mom's house back in their small town. A couple years go by, and Allison ends up getting an internship in California that she knows will help set her up to land a job post-graduation as a rising senior. Her boyfriend says he doesn't like her going that far away for the internship and that he thinks she will cheat on him being far away. She said, "Why don't you come visit me in California since you've never been, and while I'm at work you could try to network out here in the music industry." Jerry says, "It's not that easy, you have to know somebody to have a chance out there and I don't have enough money to come out." Allison booked a flight for him because she wanted him to come regardless and with this gesture, his insecurity and lack of self-confidence reached a dangerous level indicated in the conversation below:

Jerry: Stop trying to control me. I'm a man! I can take care of myself!

Allison: You are not a man. You are a boy still living at home with your mom and I cared enough to try to help you pursue your dream to give you a free place to stay. But you just don't want it bad enough and wonder why you haven't booked one solid or consistent gig in 3 years trying to do music. It's over!

Allison thought he had potential, but was wrong as hell. It was clear her ex didn't have self-confidence or a plan to be successful. Many women apparently have been in this situation and some men have that friend like Jerry who knows he just doesn't have it together and possibly never will. I wonder if Jerry would have more confidence with the problem in this next chapter...

The Oversized Ego...

"Why do some men hold on to their egos and aren't as supportive of her?"

Men are going to be men always, whatever the hell that means. There are a few things that we men do that can be deemed as wrong in a relationship that usually isn't done on purpose. One of those things is some men don't celebrate their woman's accomplishments that we didn't have a helping hand in, like we should. There have been some psychological studies that have shown men can lose a sense of manhood, self-esteem, and ego when their partner beats them in activities or makes more progress in her career than he does[4]. This unfortunately hurts his pride and will affect the romance in the relationship.

By no means am I saying a woman should ever hold herself back to cater to her man's pride and self-esteem issues. But when women express their excitement regarding her accomplishments, she should take notice to his reaction initially and shortly after. That way the issue could be addressed if he changes in any way for the negative or seems to not be excited for you.

Men are known to naturally be competitive throughout multiple aspects of life. You typically see men in drinking competitions while hanging out, food eating contest, strength ability in the weight room, who can make more money in a similar career, etc. This is one reason some men want their wives to be a housewife because it makes his ego so much stronger knowing he wears the "big drawers" in the house and he takes care of everything and everyone. If his girl was contributing to the household income significantly or making more money than him, he may look at the situation as "Yes, she's smart, beautiful, hardworking, but she

---

[4] **Dailyworth.com "What to do When He Resents your Success"-Farnoosh Torabi, March 14, 2014.**

doesn't need me if I'm not the sole provider for our lifestyle." These factors all affect how that man feels about himself, views his self-importance as a man, and what he believes the man's role is in a relationship.

Primitively, the man has been deemed the ruler and provider of his household, or "kingdom" in a sense. He typically doesn't want his queen to feel as if she is the ruler and provider. Now in modern times, it does seem that the woman will *run* the household because the term "happy wife happy life" is true... I'm nowhere near marriage, so I can't speak on it firsthand, but many men give in to please her and avoid conflict. Which, honestly, I don't think is healthy in a relationship, but that will be a topic in another chapter. As the man of the house, marriage, or relationship, he will want to know that without him, things wouldn't be the way they are. But a man who doesn't feel needed can cause psychological emotional issues--nothing extreme but how he approaches women and the kind of women he will try to attract, without being over intimidated by a woman that comes off as having very high self-esteem.

Ladies, a man who has a lot of self-esteem should be the greatest supporter of you. A man's self-esteem should not be determined by the job he has, his income, his car, or his house. If those things were taken away, he should be confident enough to get through the tough times and his ego should not be hurt. A man's ego and self-importance can be healthy when he is truly confident in who he is as a man and should enhance his relationship in the long run. A man just might need to be reminded that you're his partner and is just as important to you no matter how small or big an accomplishment seems to be of yours. Even if he had no contribution, he should support you and reward you to let you know he cares.

I had a female boss named Jamie who was dating a guy, Tyler, who worked at the company as well. One of her direct reports was a close friend of hers for many years so what they had wasn't a typical boss-employee relationship. Jamie received a promotion to an executive professional-band position which now put her two professional band levels above her boyfriend. According to Jamie's direct hire, who I was acquainted with, Jamie vented to her about how her boyfriend didn't seem that excited for her. He decided to take her to a nice dinner as a congratulatory gesture but that dinner apparently took a turn when she asked why he initially wasn't so excited.

Tyler: It just feels weird being two levels below you professionally when we are the same age.

Jamie: Is me being the woman and making more money in our relationship an issue?

Tyler: Well, I just think the man should make more in the relationship, but I am proud of you.

Ladies, how would you feel hearing that from the person you loved? I'll assume disrespected but I'll leave that up to you all for discussion.

Side Note: There's another moral of this story. Don't tell your coworkers too much about your personal relationship. I definitely shouldn't have had this information but sh*t, it came in handy for this book!

Gender Bender
"What if the roles were reversed?"

Have you ever heard a woman say, "Men don't know what we go through," or men saying, "Women think they are always right."? Have you ever thought about what would happen if the social norms of men and women were reversed? Let's just take a look at what that picture could be painted like. There are two ways I will approach this: One way is to imagine that the current social norm roles never existed and they were just reversed from the start. The second way to approach this question would be if the roles were how they are now, then reversed temporarily, and reversed back for a temporary period of time.

1st Approach:

I'm sure some of you reading this book have seen the hit movie *Think Like a Man*, based on Steve Harvey's book *Act Like a Lady, Think Like a Man*. This movie, featuring Terrence J., Kevin Hart, and many other great actors is one of the best romantic comedies movies based on a book I have seen. The book and movie have a combination of great situations where you see men and women trying to manipulate situations to cater to his or her needs in the relationship. Now imagine every situation in the movie reversed. That would change the world as we know it.

Imagine a world where a woman would make a man wait for sex, but now men make women wait for sex; men telling women "she needs to be a woman and grow up and mature;" a woman opening the car door for a man; men concerned with what they are wearing to make them not want to seem slutty or promiscuous. This would be the scariest: men asking other men to go to the bathroom during a double date or group outing to talk about only God knows what (I haven't asked any women what is discussed in the bathrooms together), and so on. There would be so many changes in the world, it would seem inhumane to live like that, from the outside looking in.

Possibly one of the two most important changes would be women having to deal with the games they have played with men. And if they had a son, would they want their girlfriend or wife to treat him like that? Another important change would be a man getting in a relationship and trying to change the woman's ways to make her the perfect woman he desires and hopes she pops the question to ask him to spend his life with her.

providing you 2 seconds to let that sink in

Yeah, I know. That's some scary sh*t right there. Let's be real. That sounds crazy! I must say, it would be even more interesting if there were a movie based on these changes. There might be one, but I haven't heard of it. I wouldn't mind getting involved in producing one. But let's stay on topic.

In the sense of roles being reversed, it would be just a regular world to an everyday life that just seems impossible. Now, let's look at the scenario above. Everything that has changed for approximately one year in the current stage of the world commencing today as you're reading this, and all these roles have changed back with all their experiences remaining in memory. Let's analyze all the changes I highlighted above and the potential end results (Feel free to respond to my social media pages at the end of the book to voice your opinion and takeaways):

1. Men Making Women Wait for Sex:

One of the greatest outcomes of this scenario would be women would understand that sex is truly a verb, not an emotion. Women would realize it's easy to have sex with someone you don't care about even while you are in love with someone else. It's just a personal choice of how you want your relationship to go. Now for us men, we would finally truly understand the women who hold their vaginas at a very high

54

standard, by not allowing penetration without a serious relationship, why it is important, how it affects your emotions, and why it is so special.

This combination of both parties being on the same page now, I believe, would result in more sex overall but it would be with higher quality people in your life. Probably 50% more men would start to value sex with someone more and probably only 5% more women would start treating sex like a verb. I believe that would be a small change because at the end of the day, sex will always be more of an emotional experience for her[5].

2. Men Telling Women to Grow Up:

This would possibly make a lot of men grow up and mature a little bit quicker with more realistic and attainable life plans. Many men who might be in a relationship with a woman and are constantly hearing the phrases "You need to grow up," "You need to be a man and handle your business," etc., would realize being a man is all about handling your responsibilities.

I do believe these would be some of the great results of this one-year exercise for those who had experienced it:

If a man has a child, he needs to work hard to have a consistent flow of income to feed his child whether he is with the mother or not. More men would stop making excuses for leading women on in relationships. He would be able to look her in the face and say, "I like you, I care about you, I'm here for you, but I'm not ready to be in a committed relationship." By doing that, he would give her an indirect ultimatum, she now knows what is going through his mind and she can

---

[5] **I pulled those figures out of nowhere.**

either stick around and hope she can change his mind, or she can leave and be free to find the next man she hopes is ready.

I will admit it. If all men handled their responsibilities, there would be a significant reduction in negative emotional outbreaks from women towards men. We wouldn't be ruining the dating experience of her for the next man after she leaves us. We would be leaving the next man to deal with an ice-cold heart that he didn't break.

3. Women Opening the Car Door for Men:

The victory in this scenario goes to the man! Women would finally realize it is not that big of a deal to open your own damn car door, especially if you have hands. More specifically, hands that work, aren't missing any fingers, and don't have torn ligaments. Ladies, would it really change the whole night and perception of a man all because he opened the car door? Him opening the car door isn't going to change his personality, how he carries himself, his goals and dreams, all his ambition or lack thereof, etc. Something that small won't make or break the relationship and shouldn't be a game changing decision as to whether you want to stick with someone or have a negative perception of him. So go ahead and reach for the door handle and open the damn door if you beat him to it. It won't change a thing.

Question: Has a woman ever said "I'm going to put up with his disrespect and inconsideration because he's gentleman enough to open my door?"

Answer: Helllllllll no!

4. Men Concerned with Their Attire to Seem Less Promiscuous:

Let's keep this response short--nothing would change. If a man can see a lot of breast, thighs, or damn near booty cheeks hanging out on the early dates, before or after this occurs, he is most likely going to see her for her body before her mind. Now if she makes him wait significantly long enough to have to get to know her and be committed, he may fall for her mind and then the body becomes the bonus, or vice versa.

5. Women Playing Games:

Women just beat the men in the Super Bowl. 100-0 is the score of this result. Women would benefit the most and more men would treat women with respect unless she truly gave him a reason not to. Most men, not all, who play games and are trying to have multiple *relationships* with women at the same damn time would start to think about their actions. They would really think about, "If this was my daughter how would I feel?".

One of the greatest hip-hop artist of all time, Nasir Jones aka "Nas," came out with a single on his *Life is Good* album entitled "Daughters." To summarize the song in one line, "They say the coolest players and foulest heartbreakers of the world, God gets us back, he makes us have precious little girls!" When a man has respect for a woman at heart, even if his actions don't always show it, he knows having a daughter would change him. And as he matures, he will treat women better without even trying, maybe.

6. Men Changing Women Hoping for a Ring:

Men would win the Gold medal for every Olympic event in this scenario's results. Women would finally understand that at the end of the day, the man chooses you, not the other way around. It doesn't even matter what religion you may potentially practice, but the largest one's all attest that a man is the one to initiate a long-term relationship/marriage. If you believe in Catholicism/Christianity, there's a verse in the Bible that states, "He who finds a wife finds a good thing and obtains favor from the Lord."-Proverbs 18:22. If you're Muslim, there's a statement in the Quran that says, "From her father to her brothers to her husband, a Muslim woman is the property of men in her life." If you practice Judaism, the Talmud, which is used to interpret the Torah, states in summary, "In all cases, the Talmud specifies that a woman can be acquired only with her consent, and not without it," Kiddushin 2a-b, indicating she is being chosen. They don't say "She who finds a husband, a man being acquired, from his sisters to his wife, he belongs to them." So remember, ladies, he chooses you and he will know if he wants to spend his life with you, regardless of what you try to change about him.

I believe the greatest outcome of reversing the roles back to how they are, is that more women would not waste time, energy, and emotions on trying to mold a man into her ideal knight in shining armor and learn to love a man and accept him for who he is, or leave him to find the man she desires. There are some women who will work so hard and even vocalize it to their friends, "I need him to stop doing this, and change the way he does this," and blah blah blah. Women would learn to accept a man for who he is, and if he wants to change his ways, he naturally will to make sure he makes her happy and will want to spend his life with her.

Ladies and gentlemen, are you ready for the role reversal experience? Probably not, just like a girl I spent time with named Jenni when I lived in Dallas. She would always complain about how I wasn't a

"Southern gentleman," but she respected my honesty. One day, over drinks by the pool:

Me: Do you want to know what it's like to be a man with what you expect of us?

Jenni: How would I do that?

Me: Let's reverse the roles for the night

Jenni: *Looks at me like I was crazy, as if I just told her to rip off her bikini, run through the city, then walk into a restaurant to order me some chicken and waffles*

Me: *Laughing* Let's flip a coin, best two out of three. Loser must court the other person for the night, including paying for the bills.

Jenni was thrilled that she had the opportunity for me to potentially pay for her and treat her how she would like for the night; because anybody who knows me can't imagine me taking somebody out on an *official social norm chivalric date*. Thank God, I called heads twice. And after two flips, she was looking very upset and distraught.

I'll shorten this story, but she ended up opening my car door, opening the restaurant door, and was checking on me to be sure my food was good since she was paying for it. After the bill was paid:

Me: What did you learn tonight?

Jenni: This is bullsh*t! I'm never agreeing to do that again. It's just weird.

Me: *Laughing* Now you see why it's not a big deal because we still had a good time out in each other's company. So don't sweat the little gestures you thought were so important.

Jenni: True but this is Texas, men raised here know how to treat a lady.

She understood the logic, which was all I cared about. If you're hoping I took her out on a date after to at least even the score, I didn't. I cooked for her though. I typically hate eating out. The portions aren't big enough for me and I'll go broke attempting to get full at a restaurant.

I just want to take the time to say thank you if you have made it this far in the book without being too angry or offended and closing it. Remember, this book is not taking shots at women or men saying what we men or what women do is wrong or right. This is just explaining the reasoning for some of men's actions. All women are strong beautiful queens.

Please remember to keep calm. I let a few people read that chapter you had just finished and give me their responses. Their blood pressure had risen. Sports is a lighter topic I believe so welcome to Sports Talk.

Sports Talk

"When the sports game is on, why do we ignore her?"

To be honest, I was surprised this question was asked so many times. I didn't realize it was such a big deal to some women. Whatever sport season the man is a big fan of, he likes to sit down, relax, have a beer, come together with the guys, and just be himself, a man, enjoying life. There are 168 hours in a week. A basketball or football game could take up to six hours out of one day, depending on tailgating and traveling to a location to watch the game. For a woman to really have an issue with the man having fun and enjoying his time without her is just a tad selfish. Actually, it's selfish as hell.

If a woman tells her man she is going out shopping, unless there are financial issues affecting their combined bank accounts, she wouldn't hear him say, "Why are you going shopping and not spending time with me?" That is your time as a woman, something you want to do with your girls to relax and enjoy your time alone if that's how you prefer to shop. The man you're interested in needs the same respect when it comes to spending downtime that makes him happy. He could be having a bad week or day, stressed out about work or family issues, etc. and "sports therapy" is equivalent to a woman's "retail therapy."

Women already control many aspects of the relationship, not because we want her to, but we just like to avoid confrontation, so let him control something. Trying to deal with her getting her way just isn't worth it at times, so we just say, "Okay" and keep it moving. During the game, women should release their power for a few hours and just go do something productive for her career, study a new sex penetration position to spice things up in their sex life, take a nap, or sit down and learn to enjoy the game with him if he is watching it by himself. Be a team player to help him be happy whether you are around him or not during a sporting event. Ladies, I could advise you to take notes from Elizabeth:

Elizabeth is a talent acquisition recruiter for a technology company in the San Francisco area. She's currently twenty-eight years old and has been dating this guy for about six to eight months. I met her when she was still single Fourth of July weekend in Vegas for an *epic* bachelor party, and we have stayed in contact frequently as friends. She sent me a comment on Snapchat one day, and I replied, "Hey what are you up to?" She informed me she had just dropped her boyfriend off at a bar to watch the hockey playoffs game. Elizabeth told me they came to an agreement that when sports are on, she would schedule something to do alone or with friends until the game was over before they would do anything together because she didn't want to be that "nagging girlfriend," wondering if the game was over and questioning what he was up to after the game. I told her that was a great strategy and great communication to avoid unnecessary confrontation. ***Let's give Elizabeth a round of applause.***

This topic leads into another question I received…

"Do men really want their women to be into sports?"

This is another one of those questions that depends solely on the individual. There are going to be only two options for the answers to this question: yes or no. There is a significant difference in the answers though, because they will probably be an indication of how he views his relationship with her in this aspect solely.

For men who say, yes, they want their women to be into sports with them, they have a very open relationship to just about any aspect of their lives. The couple shares just about everything with one another and he truly enjoys spending time with his significant other no matter what the event or activity is. This is something beautiful because typically in any relationship, both parties want their own separate time for particular activities. If he is willing to include her in what could be designated as "man time," then she should embrace it and absorb this level of quality time he wants with her.

For men who are thinking, "No, I want her to leave me alone during the game and I will begin to communicate with her when the game is over," he doesn't enjoy his lady's company as much in *that* specific aspect, not meaning he doesn't want to spend time with her. This doesn't mean he doesn't like or love her any more or less than the guy who wants his girl to enjoy the game with him. It just means that he doesn't want to spend those few hours of the day with her. It's not that big of a deal, so keep calm and carry the hell on. Now some men could end up like this guy I know Andrew, so be careful what you wish for.

Andrew once met a beautiful Southern belle who worked in IT as an analyst, like him, in New Jersey. He met her out at a bar when their rival teams were playing each other. They were tipsy and just talking trash to each other for fun. Andrew said that situation was over within a month and a half. He dropped her because "she was too into sports." I thought to myself, "How in the hell is that possible?" A lot of men would love for their women to actually know what's going on in a game if he were to take her to one for date night and she enjoys it. He said she was a huge Ole Miss football fan, and she would be on her phone during dates or group outings checking the scores of the games. I bursted out laughing at the distraught look on his face as he told me about it. He said for his next potential dating situation, he will be on high alert if he meets another girl out at a sports bar during a game who is very passionate for her team of choice.

Men Just Want Her Time

"Why do men allow the women to take control of planning activities to do together (dinner, movies, etc.)?"

When this question came up, numerous times from women surveyed, I was kind of surprised. When it comes to going out on dates, sometimes men just don't give a damn. We do not care where we go and what we do when we are with the one we care about and are proud to be seen in public with. All we probably need in this life is the one woman who makes us feel truly special. Even if the guy happens to be single (and I mean *very* single, like seen on social media with multiple girls and tags them single), there's still that one girl who he has the most feelings and values above the rest. He enjoys her company the most and will gladly let her plan their day or night together. If any man makes time to spend with you, that's the most important part--the *time* spent together, not the activity.

I believe Jay-Z said it very well in his song featuring his wife (girlfriend at the time) Beyoncé: "All I need in this life of sin, is me and my girlfriend." Most men will want to let the woman choose the activity of the day or night because at that point he values her opinion and will just want to make her smile. If she is happy in the activity she chooses, he will be happy with her. Not too many situations where the couple goes out and the man is upset about the chosen activity and it ruins the night. I know, I know, I bet at least one person who read that last sentence is thinking "That's a false ass statement because I have been on some miserable dates with my significant other!" Oh well.

If the woman is upset on a date night or at an event, it will destroy his day or night because he has to deal with the unhappy version of her. To ensure she smiles, we let her pick the details. If we end up forcing her to do something she doesn't want to do, or try to be creative to where it backfires and she doesn't appreciate the effort, we know the day or night may end without the "magic happening." And damn it, after date night and the "time is right," we are trying to give you a show like Houdini in the bedroom.

Seriously though, ladies should embrace the fact that we just want to spend time with them and not care what it is we are doing together as long as we are together. I'm sure somebody reading this right now has met someone or knows a couple who doesn't do anything at all together other than meet back at home to go to sleep. If they are happy with that situation, then it's all good, but most people wouldn't get into some form of a relationship to not spend time together outside the house at some point. If it is still an issue for a woman that her man lets her choose the activity, she should just make him choose and let him know that day or night is about him and caters to him. Hell, she should just pick the date-night details and pay for it. I guarantee he will do something special for you in the near future that is out of character or unexpected because it has made you stand out from the majority of girls who might not take it upon themselves to do that. If you're in a committed relationship, then this just ends up being bragging rights to his friends. This could allow you to grow stronger and closer together.

It would be ideal as a team whether you are married, in a relationship, or a situationship, to alternate date planning. One weekend the woman picks a date and pays for it, and the next event he pays and plans it. They cannot tell their significant other what they're doing, just let them know what time to be ready and what to wear accordingly.

An executive mentor at my first corporate job used to reach out to some of us millennials to provide us life advice. When dating or marriage came around, he said: "As soon as you young guys learn that when you let the woman do what she wants, within reason, life will be way simpler and stress free. It won't matter if you are the bread-winner or not. The woman will likely control the majority of decisions and actions, and peace in your relationship/situationship is very important." Of course, a few of us completely disagreed, but three years later still none of us are married or in serious committed relationships. Maybe by the time I write my next book, I could see personally if this was true. I would like to know my reader's views on that statement he made, whether you agree, disagree, or both.

Men and Their Female Friends

"Why do men have female friends who are attractive?"

Answering this question is going to upset many men *and* women. I apologize to the men, first, for answering this question. I know when your lady asks you about a particular "friend" who happens to be attractive, you are obligated by man code to lie just to minimize confrontation. Let me take that back--We are omitting details to avoid future problems. Since he won't be completely honest with you, I'll go ahead and air it out-- Ladies, your man is attracted to her in a physical sexual way.

There is an 85% chance (guesstimation) that when he met her, he had mental intentions or thoughts of getting to know her "physically." But there are some reasons why this would never happen, if and only if nothing ever happened. He or she might have been in a relationship when they first met. He might have tried to get to know her friend before her, or vice versa, and knew it wouldn't be a good look trying to get with somebody when you used to date their friend on some level. Or he was just too nervous to tell her how he "looked at her" and overtime decided if he hasn't said anything yet, then he might as well never say anything at all. Whichever one of these factors, or others not listed, he realized he would not cross that physical line with her and kept their relationship strictly as friends.

Some of you ladies are thinking, "There is no way in hell I want my boyfriend to be friends with a girl where if he had the chance to have sex with her in the past, he would have and still thinks about it." But this is where trust comes into play. If a man has decided to make it publicly known that he is exclusively with one woman, that should be all you need to trust him, unless you have witnessed something significant to question his loyalty and commitment to you.

The keyword in that last sentence is "witnessed." This is not an "assumption" put into your head by your insecurities or from your girlfriends who don't even know the other girl or him that well. Using strictly facts to question him will minimize the arguments started by insecure individuals. The takeaway here is...

DO NOT CREATE A STORY THAT NEVER OCCURRED!

I have a couple of situations my friend or I were a part of where attraction among friends can have multiple results highlighted above. To begin, I'll start with my friend Carl. He went to a college in Delaware, the same place the daughter of my longtime family friend went. I caught up with him a couple of years ago. When we met up, I asked if he knew her. His first reaction was, "Man she is so damn fine. If I didn't have a girlfriend when I met her, I would've had to take my chances to put myself out there to get her attention! But I have a great thing with my girl, and it wasn't worth messing up just because somebody more attractive came onto the scene." He stayed in the friend-zone with her for years and is still there even though he is now single.

I saw her when I visited Houston that summer. He saw the picture I had posted with her on social media and sent me a text to tell her hello. I did. She was glad to hear from him even though she had a boyfriend. Once she was a bit intoxicated, she said "I had a crush on him way back in the day." She's now engaged, so the timing wasn't right for them to have their moment and clearly not in fate's plan for them to be together. I'm sure this has happened many times to other people and isn't surprising.

Now my situation was different. When I was in college, I had a girlfriend during one school year, and a there was girl named Tiffany in one of my business classes. All the guys used to talk about her beauty and, I'll just be honest, she had curves in great places. We were in a group project together and somehow, someway, one day while texting, we admitted attraction. I was twenty-one years old then and a bit immature, and reflecting now at age twenty-seven, I would never do that because I know that's not appropriate or respectful to the relationship. She also had a boyfriend. Granted, we both said thanks for the compliment, and down the road, we both remained in the friend-zone.

The attraction that could've potentially lead to physical interactions, just never happened.

She is currently engaged with a two-year-old son, and we will always be friends with no problems at all when we cross paths again. Besides, she has a sister a couple years younger and taller who's a beauty as well. I ran into her at my undergrad's homecoming and we ended up having a brief, great, historical moment together. Sorry, that was honestly a random stream of thought during this session of writing this chapter. Back to the book for another topic.

Money is the Motive

"How do men feel about a woman making more money?"

This is one of those questions where the answers can vary significantly depending on the individual man. The individual will have a few opinions, using what I would call the "Dinosaur Mentality" or the "Revolutionary View."

The Dinosaur Mentality (classic gentleman) would not be a fan of this situation. I used the phrase "classic gentleman" only because it wasn't until I went to school in the South that I met quite a few men who would not want their women to make more money than them. One of the unwritten rules of manhood is to be able to provide for his family. Even though a woman can make more money and the man still provides, his pride would be hurt knowing that his woman could leave him and financially be better off than him. The classic gentleman mentality would not approve of being in this situation. Something about being "needed" for financial stability augments his ego and covers up his insecurity. Every man with this mentality wants to feel like he is Mufasa, King of the Jungle.

A man's jungle consists of his house, family, and lifestyle. Being the ruler, he wants to keep the order of how life operates within his kingdom. In a lion pride, the males look after the family and protect the territory from all enemies and the females prepare the meals and raises the kids, hunting for food and managing the cubs. I don't think the king would want to be the one in charge of preparing the meals and having his queen be the ultimate ruler and protector of the family.

Now for men who are not the classic "Southern gentlemen," and are strictly just gentleman, they will live the *Revolutionary View* and wouldn't have a problem with the woman financially bringing more to the table.

Some of you are probably wondering what the difference is between a gentleman and Southern gentleman, so let me break it down to you. A gentleman is honest and respectful. One of the definitions in the Merriam-Webster dictionary is "a man with very good manners." What is classified as bad manners is him not opening doors over time and not paying for everything from the beginning when going out on dates. The Southern gentleman is the ultimate gentleman in many people's eyes. He is the one who will not allow the woman to pay and he will always reach out for that door to open it for her even if she beats him to it.

To me, whether you are the "Dinosaur Man" or the "Revolutionary Man," it will be important for the man to stay a man by handling his business as the protector and remaining the king of his jungle. That isn't just financially. Being a man is not making excuses and taking responsibility for all his actions and decisions whether they work out for better or worse. The man's income should not be the deciding factor of his status, who he is, or what he must bring to the relationship.

When I was moving to Chicago, the moving company sent a group of guys. One of the workers, an older guy named Joe, and I got into a casual conversation:

Joe: Are you living the single life up in your youth?

Me: I am. You must be in a relationship.

Joe: I'm married to the greatest wife on Earth. Her independence is what kept my attention. She is in a managerial position working at a financial services company.

Me: **I'm thinking his wife is possibly bringing more money into the house**

Joe: She makes more than me and we have a joint account for the main bills, a retirement account, and our own personal accounts for whatever we want to spend on. The girls I dated in the past came off as if they were just trying to live off my income and that brought on stressful and difficult conversations that led to break-ups.

Me: In someone's eyes you hit the lotto because I can tell you this-- women who work in financial services in finance, risk, or accounting functions tend to be very organized with their finances and will make more money than the average person for their geographical location. It is the nature of the industry to be able to pay better compared to other industries.

Joe: Man, I'm feeling extra blessed now that I married her knowing that information.

It was a good laugh if you heard the way he said it in his heavy country accent. There are some men who have a different reaction though.

Meet Ronnie. Ronnie was somebody I met in college and I ran into him when I moved here to Atlanta. We were out at the bars in the Buckhead area, and he asked:

Ronnie: Hey how's the book progressing? I have been following the social media and seen updates about it over the years. Your book idea had me thinking some things I was taught growing up may have me missing out on great women.

Me: Oh word, what do you mean?

Ronnie: My father told me that as a man, you're the provider of the house when you grow up and a woman shouldn't make nearly as much money as you because a man takes cares of the bills and should be the sole provider.

Now Atlanta, GA currently has a high volume of women. According to the Atlanta Journal Constitution's Adam Carson, as of February 2015 there were 80,000 more single women ages eighteen to sixty-four in Atlanta than single men. With great statistics like that and the many different thriving industries in Atlanta, a man can easily meet a woman with a job that pays well above the national average income. I guess some of the women Ronnie met were making more than him and he

72

couldn't mentally get past the thought of her making more than he did as a part-time personal trainer and football coach. I told him that sounds a bit more insecure than holding on to what his father taught him, but he should do what's best for him.

Want Her, Got Her, Drop Her

"Why do men get her to go all in just to let her go?"

I'll be completely honest. A lot of men, not all but some likely in their "boy" stage (very immature and completely full of crap days), have done this at least once in their lifetime. I can say I was typically straightforward with girls, but I had to make girls feel like it was going somewhere when I knew I didn't want any potential long-term commitment. The cause for these actions really were never thought about. I know the reason though, I wanted to get buns (sex) from her and didn't think I would like her. I was just living in the moment playing games. Unfortunately, I never thought about how she was going to feel after it was over with. After I was asked this question, I had to think back on some of the many different motivational factors for these actions.

Before the woman allows herself to be emotionally available, she must understand it's all a risk that he may let her go. Even without crossing the physical line some guys are just going through the motions and will make up a bullsh*t reason not even knowing why they had the situation end. For the men who know what they are looking for, these are some of the factors/events that weigh in on his decision to leave:

1. Sexual Activity:

If a man is benefiting sexually from the dating/pre-relationship stage early on, that could possibly be a factor for why he may leave you. He could be satisfied in that aspect, but you haven't fulfilled his non-sexual needs. It's a good chance the physical attraction was the original motive to be in contact with you. He may have had that pleasure before he really knew you as a person, and then his time with you outside of that aspect isn't quite as meaningful.

Keep in mind, ladies, if you feel like you were this victim before, that doesn't mean you are not worth committing too. That just means he wasn't the one for you. Next time let him fall for who you are before he gets the physical benefits. It will significantly increase the chances of the situation growing into something real or at least more than just a physical connection.

2. 3rd Party Entourage:

Who knows the details of your current situation? If a woman tells her family, closest friends, co-workers, social media community, etc. regarding time with the new guy she is talking to or dating, and he knows that you're giving everyone too many details. He may start to think, "I don't want everyone in my business so soon when we aren't even official! I think it's time to start my exit."

Ladies, if you believe you have been in this situation and still are single, the next time you start the pre-dating stages with a guy, shut the hell up and wait for the situation to grow to an exclusive commitment before you start telling the world. Minimize the chances of him making you think you're deeper into dating than you guys are and him leaving without questioning his decision.

3. Scared of Change:

Usually when a man starts to truly like a woman, he will naturally change. The changes can range from an increase in time spent with her, sending her the goodnight text and nobody else, to actually being seen in-public together after they have started having sex. When these things happen, he will embrace it and try to see where it goes, or he will get nervous and make up an excuse to end the situation.

This is somebody who just wasn't ready and the idea of being with one person until the end of time was too much to handle. Ladies, that means you have significant qualities as a woman that only a strong and secure man can handle. You will become the "One That Got Away," and he will regret it. But again, that means he wasn't the one. Everybody you date is a lesson or a blessing, or a combination of both. Don't worry. The right one for you is never going to leave you, so don't settle when that guy comes crying back wanting another chance. Tell him, "I'm moving." He will ask, "Where to?" And you can say, "On to better things!"

4. One Girl or Two Girls or More:

Sometimes, unfortunately, the man might not be completely honest with her about his feelings or sometimes there is someone else in the picture she doesn't know about. I have witnessed and personally have been in a situation where guys are dating two girls and after a month or two of spending time with both, one girl might be favored over the other. So, he starts to drift away from the other. And she won't know unless he decides to make it public on social media or grows a solid set of balls and tells her what's really happening.

If you ever felt like you weren't the only one in the picture, and you have some concrete evidence of this (don't over think it), walk away from that situation if the trust is completely gone. That's very disrespectful to not be straightforward about it, especially if he is physically involved with you both. Hopefully he would apologize, but that doesn't mean he deserves a second chance any time soon. Stay strong and decide your value.

5. <u>Just Looking for Fun</u>:

There are some men who are at a point in their lives where they don't want a relationship but they also don't want exclusivity, just looking for that happy medium that's right in-between. He ends up meeting someone to spend time with, and talking to her makes all his personal issues temporarily disappear, which is all he needs--somebody to keep his mind off the negativity and keeps him focused on the goals he is hopefully working toward. The biggest issue is he probably didn't communicate the way he viewed their time together, and she probably didn't communicate how she viewed it as well.

The miscommunication has clearly occurred and at some point, the discussion is going to turn into an argument. He might be bold and say, "I don't want a relationship right now in my life!" Ladies, please keep calm and listen to the exact words that he said. I repeat: Pay attention to the exact words he used. Sometimes women take what we say and hear something completely different such as--"He said he doesn't want a relationship from me like I'm not worth commitment!" This is not what he said. He simply means he isn't ready for commitment to *anybody*, but he doesn't want to be with multiple women at the same time either. He liked what you had, but if that's not what you were looking for, don't settle. Let him go. Keep your standards as high as you believe they are.

At the end of the day, all five of these potential factors could make a man leave after you have fallen hard if he wasn't ready at the beginning. So, ladies, do not look down on yourself when a man decides to leave after a short amount of time. Just know that he wasn't ready or mature, and he probably didn't communicate that effectively to you. There will always be someone else out there for you.

The most important thing to do after an emotional situation ends with someone is to not get yourself involved with another man until your heart, mind, and soul is cleared from the previous man. The new guy might be trying to be serious, so don't ruin it for him because now that you aren't ready because of the last guy. It's a horrible recycled system of events.

Wendy is a thirty-year-old, beautiful curly-haired woman who is a pharmacist in Phoenix. I met her at a bar in Old Town Scottsdale a few years ago. She had an interest in me until I said I was not looking for any potential dating situation. She said, "At least you're man enough to know that." Curiosity struck. Why did she say that? What happened? Wendy told me about a guy she knew through a friend who took her on a date some years ago. Their chemistry was greater than she anticipated. A couple months go by, and now he's saying emotional ass statements like, "I'm truly glad I asked you out because you're incredible. You have the long-term qualities I haven't seen yet in a woman." She was hopeful that her single life would be done forever! Two more months go by and his statements have changed--- "I'm not quite sure I'm ready for this. Should we take a step back?" She said things were great physically, publicly, and just seemed to be going in a great direction until his communication started to dwindle. After the fling officially ended, he said he meant what he said but realized he wasn't ready to give up the single life. At first, she believed it was another woman (FYI: She has no proof. This is a theory she created in her head). She concluded it was not another girl later when their mutual friend confirmed he wasn't dating anybody else. Wendy has been single for the past two years since her last fling. Tough.

It Looks/Smells/Sounds/Feels/Taste Like a Relationship… But It's Not?

"Why do men want to do every activity with her, but won't give her the title?"

Just to keep things clear, this question and its response is made for the men and women who have been in these exclusive dating pre-title relationships for four months or longer. Let's call them "high-end situationships." Anything before four months...keep calm it's still early. This topic is for those who have been with someone so long that you can do, have done, or are currently doing the following:

- Spend the night so much you may have your own toothbrush there or always have one on you.

- You have gone out with each other's friends.

- All your friends know that you are together with no title.

- Have been introduced to family members during a special occasion (not necessarily holidays but maybe a family barbecue or someone's birthday dinner).

- Gone on any sort of vacation together and people knew about it via social media (Doesn't mean a thing if you go on vacation and keep it a secret, right?)

Some women do all this, and they've been exclusive emotionally and physically four months or longer with no title and don't understand why. Ladies, do not ever let the idea of, "Am I not worth the girlfriend title?" creep up in your mind or let friends/relatives put that in your mind. If you weren't worth it, he wouldn't have done all the above with you and made it public. It is simply because we know that when there is a title change, sometimes relationship dynamics between us will change and it is scary as hell.

I know of couples who don't have the title for a long time, and if the female party decides to do something drastic, like making it "Facebook official" without the man's prior knowledge, he will calmly shrug it off and think nothing of it. Or he will feel blindsided and send a mass text to his closest friends in a group chat freaking out. Trust me, I've seen it happen, and that group chat was very entertaining. It started with, "Why would she do that? This is the beginning of the end!"

I know some of the women will say, "It isn't a big deal because everyone knew about us being *us*." But that's when you need to communicate to him that the title doesn't mean things are going to change for the worst, only get better with the titled security. Most men have seen how some people's relationships go downhill because the title came and the woman didn't realize she was changing and becoming more demanding with the title. Ladies, just know that when you receive the title, whether it's his decision or yours, you both need to have a mutual understanding that the title means you are trying to make progress for the future. It is imperative that you start to show him he made the right decision. Hard to swallow, but it's time to potentially start catering a bit more to his needs to make him as comfortable as possible with this next step in the relationship.

I'm not saying go crazy and spend money you don't have on him or put gifts on the credit card. But if you know he has a favorite food, cook it for him. For you ladies with a lack of cooking capabilities, take him to dinner. If he has a favorite sports team and its local, depending on the financial situation, treat him to a game just because or buy some memorabilia for when he is watching the games. Anything to show him that he should not second guess things and the title should stick for a little while at least.

I have a close acquaintance named Chelsea. She is a beautiful loving person. She moved to South Carolina from New Jersey years ago for a change from the lifestyle and environment she was raised in, and while there she met a guy named Chris. Chris works in accounting for a company an hour away from her. They went on dates and started sleeping together and developed a significant comfort to be on social media together. Over a year went by and she hadn't received a title. She would tell him her feelings on the subject and she would even attempt to pressure him by threatening to end what they had going on since he admitted he wasn't ready for commitment. A few more years go by. The times when Chelsea and I caught up she would say, "I'm moving on, he just isn't ready." Then she would keep falling for what her heart was telling her--to stick with him still because she loves him and he loves her too, apparently.

They've been on international trips together now and have met family members, but he still hasn't committed to her officially. The heart wants what the heart wants, but damn. It's literally been four years! Yes, four years of being in love with no official commitment. She even admitted he could be sleeping with another woman, "but I know I only do it with him because he is all I want." I personally hope she starts to hold herself up to higher standards, but it could be too late. I told her if I ever met that dude I would tell him to commit to her or leave her alone altogether. Stop holding this woman back from being a blessing to someone else. Psych, that isn't my business to do that. We are grown ass adults and must live with our decisions. Overall, Chris has gotten comfortable and knows he doesn't need the title to do relationship-activities, so he is holding on for as long as he can.

No matter what happens, when a woman receives the official title, she shouldn't become more controlling and think he must change anything he is currently doing. Aren't you trying to get him to the point that he feels like he can't live his life without you and put a ring on it? Most importantly, if you have to strategize how to get him to commit, I don't believe he wants to commit.

What Have You Done for Me Lately?

"Why do men stop doing the little things they did at the beginning of the relationship?

There are many women in relationships, whether they are dating, engaged, or married, who seem to have a phrase that indicates the current level of commitment on display isn't enough: "You don't do the things you use to do for me anymore. We don't go out as much as we use to at the beginning." And apparently, this is the man's fault. No man will ever tell a woman, "I'm taking you out so I can potentially make you mine and once you are mine, I have achieved my goal and don't feel the need to take you out anymore. I did this to get you, not to keep you." Most men don't want to truly take a lady out and spend his money that way. The unwritten laws are men must court women, be *gentleman* (keep in mind our discussion earlier about this definition), and pay for the first dates to show that he is interested. Well remember, if you believe that last sentence, he did it to show he is interested, not because he wants to do that. Here is an example that I'm sure will offend somebody, but it is the truth.

Most young men who grew up in the video games era have at some point in their life owned or played the game Grand Theft Auto. For those of you who do not know the game, it is a game where you are a character who starts off as a nobody. You commit crimes and gain money, power, and respect. This game has many levels and missions. Once you have completed them all, you have achieved the status of the biggest crime lord and "own the streets." It is the same way with women.

At the beginning we are a nobody, we are just a stranger who you're not sure wants something real or not. Now to gain your trust, we must complete multiple missions--take you out on dates to see if there's a common interest or to keep attention. We decide to take you out again, another mission, which now has the trust and respect level earned that he may get to know you physically, evidence of our status being elevated. And he is now a true somebody on his way to the top of the ranks. Once he has her completely exclusive and committed ("owns the streets"), he doesn't have to put in the same level of work from the beginning. The new title as a "crime lord/boss," or boyfriend, means certain things aren't necessary anymore. Is Mark Zuckerberg still doing the foundation work for Facebook?

Sorry, ladies, but it is the truth. He never wanted to do that courting thing but he did what he had to do to get what he wanted. I want all of you beautiful strong women to know it is not your fault. You didn't do anything wrong but have an expectation based on what we did at the beginning and wanted that to be the minimum standard. This is where all men, boys, and gentleman have really, really, *really* messed up to be honest.

To my fellow brothers of the man species, I advise you to stop setting the dating standard so high at the beginning. Once you reach the goal of having her whether it's physically or for a commitment, majority of you fall off. If we set the dating standards very low at the beginning, then her expectations are lower and we can gradually build our way up to show improvement. By setting standards lower at the beginning, I'm not suggesting that we should take you for snacks at the Dollar Store and just look at each other in the car or house talking. Take her or meet her somewhere that's free and public. A lot of women truly enjoy these things for dates. Men, remember to eat a thorough meal before you go on that "free" date, because if you get hungry in front of her, you don't want to come off as rude and order yourself some food without offering her anything, just a #FryesFinancialTip[6] suggestion. If a man needs to spend a lot of money consistently to attract someone, then you better keep it going after you have her attention, or else you will have this chapter's topic conversation. Let's just look at one of the most famous athletes of all time and how their careers relate to this scenario.

Imagine if Michael Jordan won most of his championships at the beginning of his career and then the last six or seven seasons he didn't win one MVP,

---

[6] A future book related to saving money with someone you're interested in getting to know

championship, or all-star appearance. We would've viewed his career differently. Most great athletes reach their prime years after they have been in the pros. Same concept applies to a relationship. Everything should get better gradually in a relationship, situationship, or whatever your status is with a significant other.

Over the years the dates, the sex, the conversations, the adventures, should get better until you two as a couple have reached the retirement stage, and by that, I mean you physically can't do the same things you used to when you were younger. Hopefully this occurs after marriage, kids, and/or grandkids come into your lives if that is something you planned on together. I keep referring to agreements and having an understanding as a couple because at the end of the day, it is two of you in the relationship so be on the same page for expectations from one another.

If you met my friend Monica and heard her story, her boyfriend is a prime example of someone who was ready to put in all the work he needed strictly to get her attention exclusively. I met Monica through a group chat in Atlanta, and we became close friends. We caught up over drinks and of course, given we are at that age people are curious about dating life, she told me somebody she met on a dating app met her at the park for their first outing. Then he took her to dinner. Then he cooked for her. Then she took them to the movies, and they really enjoyed each other's company. He asked her to be his girlfriend and she was excited thinking how lucky she was to meet a guy with a real job who was also a gentleman.

Her first birthday in the relationship came around, and he had Edible Arrangements sent to her job with flowers and a balloon. That evening, they did a wine tasting and a make-your-own-food combination event. She was glad he was thoughtful and he didn't just take her to dinner like a regular night. He apparently did something *special* for Valentine's Day as well. Fast forward one year later, and Valentine's Day rolls around again. This dude made last minute reservations for a restaurant the day before Valentine's Day. They were stuck with a 10:00PM reservation. He didn't send anything to her job or have something to surprise her with at home. He didn't even set plans to do anything before they went to dinner, it was just him picking her up at 9:30 to go eat, and they didn't have sex after.

She vented this to me:

Monica: I think he has become really comfortable because he doesn't put thought into anything anymore.

Me: Are you going to leave him because he isn't as thoughtful anymore for dates and your time together?

Monica: Of course not.

Me: *Laughing* He knows that as well. That's why I keep that dating bar low at first.

Monica: Shut up, you're just a cheap ass.

Me: Either way, he did exactly what he thought he needed to do to get you, but he was never told to keep up that pace to keep you. So you need to communicate with him what you're telling me. It does you absolutely no good just talking about him to other people.

It's been eight months since then, and she still hasn't truly told him what she vented to me. She said she hinted towards what she meant to say and I wished her good luck. It's on her at this point to do what she needs to be happy.

Now You See It, Now You Don't

"Why does he have to lose her to realize what he had?"

This question isn't directly just for men. There are many women who have made the same mistake of taking the person they are dating for granted. Not truly appreciating everything they do for them, whether it's being supportive of career or academic goals, helping them out financially when the partner hits a rough patch, cooking dinner for the other, or taking them out on a date after one has had a rough day or week--it is human nature sometimes to do this for two reasons:

1.   He/She might not be ready for that relationship.

2.   His/Her exposure to dating experiences.

Let me break these two reasons down for you a little more.

When an individual is completely ready, they will naturally appreciate the things that their partner will do for them. Everything from cooking, cleaning, supporting, being engaged with their goals, respecting family members they might not get along with, random gestures of affection, etc. I believe people get a relationship twisted when they think that a relationship's main goal is to be faithful and committed to being with him/her. That is literally the basics and the bare minimum. Feel free to let me know on the website what you value most from someone else you're with.

When someone is truly ready and committed, you are committed to every aspect of that person's life to help them grow and make progress in life. As the support system of this life long journey you are pursuing, one should always count the pros and cons of the person. If the pros outweigh the cons significantly, remember there are some individuals who have the opposite scenario from their partner so count your blessings.

If he or she isn't ready for the long run and they lose that person--when they start to second guess their decision to let that person go--that's when they become ready and realized they missed out on a great person. They will take that lesson and learn from it to be more prepared for the future.

For the second reason, sometimes individuals don't realize how good they have it until the next person they date is just a monster who makes them want to run back to the past. They might have messed things up with them for life. For example, you have a job and heard your competitor pays slightly better and has an open position. So, you decide to jump ship. Now you are at the new company and your boss is now micro-managing you. After a few months, you realized the grass wasn't greener on the other side.

Ladies, you might have had the man who was not the most ambitious or consistent with dates. You leave him and this new guy takes you on dates all the time and gets you gifts, but he is disrespectful and becomes verbally or physically abusive. Then you try to run back to the past only to find that they have already moved on and it is too late. Another lesson learned.

It's all about if you are *satisfied with* your partner or *settling for* your partner. Never settle for someone. That will just destroy you as a person in the long-run and leave you filled with regret. You must make sure this person provides you with what you need, not just what you want.

A brief example about this is my friend's brother named Brian. Brian was enjoying the single life for years. He met a woman out who he thought was the most beautiful thing on Earth. She would cater to him and she had a great career starting, so he began courting her. They did the dating without any official commitment for over a year. She eventually got fed up and said, "Commit to me, or I'm gone." He said he was too focused on his career to be worried about a relationship. She dropped him like a sack of potatoes. Two years later, she got engaged to another man and now Brian believes she was the one, and he threw it all away. He made a mistake, but that's how people grow. You learn from the mistake, so when the next opportunity comes around you'll be good to go early on for the long-run. I wonder how many readers who are currently single think they messed up and missed out on "the one." Or do they think that lesson was needed in life to be prepared for who may be the one in the future?

Social Media Cannot Ruin a Relationship...
"Why don't some men like to promote their relationship on social media?"

As of 2015, the amount of information we as humans put on the Internet via social media would seem scary to the baby boomers if they were nearly as active in it as us millennials. Included in this information overload provided on social media are our personal lives, unnecessary negative personal events, and relationship statuses. Originally when modern social medias like MySpace and Facebook began, it was always the right thing to do if you were in a relationship with someone to make it publicly known by keeping the relationship status updated. Over a fairly short period of time, some individuals started to believe it was a good idea to do one of the following:

1. Be in a relationship and then block it from the public view on social media.

2. Be in a relationship and try to avoid being seen together in public.

3. Be in a relationship and have it for public view on social media, but block certain individuals from being able to see it.

4. Be in a relationship but never post anything in the slightest that indicates they are in a relationship.

Sometimes Number 4 will happen where both parties agree to not let the public know they are together. Only their closest personal friends and family who are witnessing anything know the truth of their commitment to one another. What women and men need to understand is that if there isn't ANY public indication via social media, it leaves the door wide open for temptation to walk in.

It does seem that in a relationship, in general, you will witness the woman posting more pics or statuses regarding her significant other than her man. I believe as long as the man does some type of public social media promotion indicating that he is taken using phrases or words such as "my girl," "my love," or plain and simple "HER" is a beautiful thing. Now if the guy isn't really on social media and barely does a random post a month, then I wouldn't overthink it. But if he posts about his new job, new car, new watch, partying with friends, and just so happens to not post anything regarding his relationship--red flag because people post what they value to show others. Something that small says, "This woman is someone I'm with and not afraid to show it." Unfortunately, some men just will not do this.

I'm excluding professional athletes and celebrities from this as they live an extremely different lifestyle from the majority.

If a woman asks her man, "Why don't you ever promote me, post pics of us or me, or give me any acknowledgement on social media?" Again, especially if he uses social media on a regular basis, his response might be "I don't want people in my business," or "social media can ruin things between us so I think it's better to not be on display." This is just straight up bullsh*t. It's a 99.9% chance he is entertaining other girls on the side who text or call him. Alright, I over exaggerated that guesstimation percentage, but you get the point. If a man is completely committed to you and does not want to entertain any other woman in the slightest way of communication, he has nothing to hide and should never have an issue with being on display with his lady.

Now I know some women's responses might be, "Well if other girls see that picture they might start texting him or calling him trying to see what's going on with this relationship to get attention." This is true. Other girls may become jealous and may try to test the waters of the relationship. Keep in mind ladies if you are willing to try to interrupt someone's relationship, don't be surprised if karma comes back and tries to interrupt yours whether you know it or not. When a third party tries to interrupt a couple, it is the partner's responsibility to immediately do one of the following actions:

1. Block all forms of contact with the outsider whether it is social media or by phone.

2. Politely ask the third party to respect your relationship and avoid contacting you if they continue to contact you in a way your partner would find inappropriate.

3. If Option 2 fails, then proceed with option 1 and make the decision on letting your partner know what has occurred.

*Another suggestion: If it was an extremely quick turnaround (one week or less) from the time you receive inappropriate message from the third party and blocking all forms of contact, don't say anything to your partner and proceed with your relationship/situationship like it never happened.

Social media cannot ruin a relationship. Only the person allowing themselves to entertain this third party's comments, messages, likes, pokes, and emoji's[7] is the reason for the interruption. Anyone who entertains the third party clearly is not ready for an exclusive committed relationship with you because if they did, they would have followed one of the three options above without hesitation. If a man/woman considers cheating, they would've always considered it whether it came from someone on social media, a coworker, an old "friend", a random girl/guy they met on a business trip, etc. it was their decision. How many people that cheated on someone or have been cheated on believe "if there was no social media, I wouldn't have cheated or wouldn't have been cheated on?"

Men, imagine this: Your girlfriend is traveling a lot for work and both of you live in Chicago. Her company takes her to Boston almost monthly for business. Before you got into a relationship, your girlfriend told you she had a "friend with benefits" in Boston from the past. She assures you now that you both are committed; her former booty call is not an issue and you decide to trust her word.

One day she's showing you something on her phone and she gets up to leave the room briefly and a direct message from a guy pops up on her phone saying, "Hey are you still in Boston?" Now you have these questions sprinting through your head:

- Who the f**k is he?

- Why is he sending her a DM?

- Why is he asking about her whereabouts?

You immediately bring it up to your girlfriend and she responds snappy with the explanation of, "That's an old friend. We haven't slept together for years. He must've seen a post I had at the restaurant and doesn't have my phone number." Now if you have no proof she is lying you shouldn't yell and fight about it. Only thing you do know is that she hasn't posted any photos of you on social media but you have posted pics with her. There is a chance that if she would've had pictures of ya'll together, this other man never would've sent the message.

Now my friend Michelle and her boyfriend Ted's situation is a little different. In this example, the guy is more like Michelle and the girlfriend has Ted's actions. Now Michelle is insecure because Ted took a promotion that is moving him to Boston where his former flings are probably looking forward to catching up with him again to see if he is single or not. With her boyfriend's bad communication this made her feel uncomfortable with the situation. She ended up dumping him as soon as she saw his picture tagged with a girl and his hands were lower on her waist than she liked. After being in a relationship for over a year where he hadn't made one post with her and he was posting other things…it looks shady and now the relationship is over.

To any man or woman who believed that social media ruined your relationship or prevented it from going anywhere long-term due to outside individuals, slap yourself at least twice for me. The relationship just wasn't meant to be if that person or yourself allowed "C" to get between "A and B." Remember, the dude put his hands around her, whether it was on or off camera.

Here's the Truth

I would like to thank you for making it to the end of this book. Now that you have read a new perspective of why men do or say certain things I just want to provide a one-liner response from the question/chapters you've read to summarize:

1. Why do men freak out about commitment?
He didn't expect to get to a point of readiness to commit exclusively and publicly.

2. When does a man know if he is ready for a relationship?
If a man truly knows himself well, he will be able to answer that question.

3. What characteristics push a man away immediately?
Every man is different and there are some common reasons that will push men away. His tolerance level for that reason will vary based on life experiences.

4. How will she know if he is really interested?
This is an individual case-by-case basis, but if people close to him (friends, family, co-workers) tell you he's acting differently with you in a good way, then that's a great sign.

5. If he waits for sex, is it because it's real or patience for penetration?
Unfortunately, she won't know until it happens. (Hope for the best if you do not want to wait until marriage for sex).

6. Why do men like easy sex over a girl with values?
If that's the man's objective of what he is looking for, then he will go find it.

7. How often does sex cross a man's mind?
A lot.

8. Why do men like to rush into sex?
Reference the answer to question 6.

9. How should a woman tell her man he is not satisfying her sexually?
Just don't say it in a humiliating way and keep it between you two about his "performance," unless you both agree to seek professional sex counseling.

10. Why are men insensitive?
Ehh, some are and some aren't. No right answer.

11. Why don't men talk about and express their feelings?
This is a communication issue on an individual basis.

12. Why are men bad at communicating?
Reference the answer to question 11.

13. Why are men passive listeners?
Reference the answer to question 12.

14. Why don't men tell their woman that they just need alone time without shutting down?
Reference the answer to question 13.

15. Why aren't men very assertive with their life decisions?
Very individualized basis answer, but life experiences will shape this typically.

16. Why do some men hold on to their egos and aren't as supportive of her?
This is either a self-confidence issue, thinking he is in competition with her, unintentionally on an individual case-by-case basis.

17. What if the roles were reversed?
Men and women in general would possibly begin to understand each other but until then... good luck.

18. When the sports game is on, why do we ignore her?
It's called enjoying his damn time temporarily without you so keep calm.

19. Do men really want their women to be into sports?
Some do, some don't. Depends on what he prefers.

20. Why do men allow the women to take control of planning activities to do together?
He wants to spend time with you and the details don't matter.

21. Why do men have female friends who are attractive?
If they're strictly just friends, don't even ask this question. Just know he would penetrate her under proper conditions and circumstances. Cheating on you is NOT one of those conditions/circumstances.

22. How do men feel about a woman making more money?
Individually based answers, but he is insecure as hell if he has an issue with her making more money than him.

23. Why do men get her to go all-in just to let her go?
He liked her but wasn't ready for the real thing. Sorry if that has happened to you.

24. Why do men want to do every activity with her, but won't give her the title?
He's enjoying all forms of time spent with her, but again, he isn't ready for the real thing.

25. Why do men stop doing the little things they did at the beginning of the relationship?
He did it to get you. Now he accomplished the goal. Operation Chill Out has commenced for him (LOL just kidding but you get the point).

26. Why does he have to lose her to realize what he had?
Most people don't appreciate something beneficial until it's not available anymore. Same concept.

27. Why don't some men like to promote their relationship on social media?
If he is usually posting on social media but not posting you, he's too private about dating or hiding something/someone.

I hope you have been entertained, had a few laughs, been able to relate to the personal stories I've shared, and perhaps considered some of the decisions you've made related to the dating, relationships, and situationships you may be going through. Most importantly, I hope you've gained an understanding of why men do or say certain things in different situations from my non-emotional, strictly logical, millennial individual's male perspective. In no way, shape, or form are you wrong if you disagree with anything I stated. I'm inviting you to leave comments in the blog and the link on the following page that allows you to become a member of the worldwide book club on my website to discuss your notes from each chapter with other book readers for a friendly dialogue.

About the Author

Ariston Teleo is an alias name. The name is derived from the Greek phrase "The Best Execute/Finish/Complete." He is a millennial from the Kansas City area. He was inspired to write this book and it took him a total of 5 years from the very first outline of questions to the point it is now available for sale. He was 23 years old when he started this book journey and now 28 years old when this book is released. He wants you to know that this book is only the beginning of him making his name and look out for future books!

The next section is for you to write any notes or thoughts you had while reading this book as you reflect on what you read.

Feel free to share your thoughts on the author's website in the "Blog" section or send him a private message in the "Ask the Author" section.

Notes

STAY CONNECTED

Read more about the author and future books:

www.AristonTeleo.com

Follow the author's social medias:

facebook.

https://www.facebook.com/AristonTeleo/

Instagram

@iAmAriston

twitter

@AristonTeleo

Thank You